Finding the
Right One
After
Divorce

Edward M. Tauber
& Jim Smoke

HARVEST HOUSE PUBLISHERS

EUGENE, OREGON

Unless otherwise indicated, Scripture quotations are taken from The Message. Copyright © by Eugene H. Peterson 1993, 1994, 1995, 1996, 2000, 2001, 2002. Used by permission of NavPress Publishing Group.

Verses marked NKJV are taken from the New King James Version. Copyright ©1982 by Thomas Nelson, Inc. Used by permission. All rights reserved.

Verses marked NLT are taken from the *Holy Bible*, New Living Translation, copyright ©1996. Used by permission of Tyndale House Publishers, Inc., Wheaton, IL 60189 USA. All rights reserved.

Cover by Terry Dugan Design, Minneapolis, Minnesota

Cover photo © Anthony Harvie/Photodisc Red/Getty Images

FINDING THE RIGHT ONE AFTER DIVORCE
Copyright © 2007 by Edward M. Tauber and Jim Smoke
Published by Harvest House Publishers
Eugene, Oregon 97402
www.harvesthousepublishers.com

Library of Congress Cataloging-in-Publication Data
Tauber, Edward, 1943-
  Finding the right one after divorce / Edward M. Tauber and Jim Smoke.
    p. cm.
  Includes bibliographical references.
  ISBN-13: 978-0-7369-1936-4 (pbk.)
  ISBN-10: 0-7369-1936-8
  1. Remarriage--Religious aspects--Christianity. 2. Mate selection--Religious aspects--Christianity. 3. Marriage--Religious aspects--Christianity. 4. Divorce--Religious aspects--Christianity. I. Smoke, Jim. II. Title.
  BV838.T38 2007

  248.8'46--dc22

                        2006030634

Printed in the United States of America

07 08 09 10 11 12 13 14 15 / BP-CF / 10 9 8 7 6 5 4 3 2 1

Contents

❧ ❧ ❧

Introduction

※ ※ ※

Okay, you're divorced. Are you ready to move on? To start dating? To contemplate finding the right one for you? To consider remarriage? Some of us who divorce are afraid to try it again. We don't trust our own judgment. Others are so eager to find someone they race out and hook up with the first prospects who come along. Whether you're hiding out from the opposite sex, on a mission to remarry, or somewhere in-between, you need to know the facts.

First the good news. About 80 percent of divorced people do remarry. Many of the 20 percent who don't, stay single by choice. So the task of finding *someone* to remarry is not insurmountable. Now the bad news. The challenge is finding the *right one*. More than 40 percent of remarriages end in another divorce. Remarriages that fail last an even shorter time than terminated first marriages. And some of the "successful" remarriages are because the people want to avoid a repeat divorce. Sadly, government statistics reveal that the rate of divorce and redivorce is no different for Christians than for the rest of the population.

As you can see, there is a reason we didn't title this book "Finding *Someone* After Divorce." Most divorced people already accomplish that. What many do not accomplish is finding the right one. This book takes you through the primary reasons remarriages fail and reveals what you can do to help make your next marriage successful.

The valuable information we present is based on our more than 35 years of combined experience working in the counseling and divorce recovery fields, personal experience, an extensive independent survey of divorced people, and government statistics.

Ed's Story

I've been very successful in most aspects of my life. I earned a Ph.D. from an Ivy League school. I was a full professor at a prestigious university. I had an industry career as a research director for major corporations. I had a profitable consulting practice. I was able to retire at the age of 43. I have lots of friends. My parents loved me. And I didn't have a dysfunctional family while growing up. My life has been, generally speaking, very good. The one area where I didn't succeed—in fact, I failed dismally—was marriage.

Yes, I am a recovered divorceaholic. I've been married several times. After my last divorce, I decided to do something different. I studied the reasons why I and so many other people divorced. I wanted to know the primary causes of redivorce and how divorced people can have happy remarriages.

I discovered that if you want to find the right person to marry, you have to avoid the pitfalls that divorce creates and learn from your past experiences. If you remarry when you're not ready, you dramatically increase the risk of getting another divorce. In fact, you'll likely marry the wrong person for the wrong reasons and eventually find your dreams shattered once again. And it's not any easier in a repeat divorce than it is in the first one. I know from experience. I don't want you to go through what happened to me. I want to share with you what I've learned about gauging how to know when you're ready to remarry and when you're not—and what you can do to find the right person to love.

Here's the promise of this book for you if you're divorced or one of the redivorced: *Spend a few hours reading and understanding what happened to me and to many others, and you'll increase the odds of finding the right one for you and reduce the chance of another divorce.*

I think you'll find our message ultimately hopeful and helpful.

Whether you have been divorced once, twice, or more times than you want to talk about, you can learn a lot from the mistakes trotted out on these pages. How do I know? I know for sure because today I am very happily married, and I'm sure I will never be divorced again. I accomplished this successful marriage by studying *what went wrong* previously and acting on the insights I learned. What I gained from this journey into my past motivated me to write this book so you can avoid my mistakes and the mistakes of others.

As I reviewed my less-than-blissful wedded history, I saw recurring themes. I was so distraught after each divorce that I made bad choices out of neediness and desperation. I wanted someone else to solve my problems and fix my loneliness. I never gave myself time to heal and become independent. Maybe these marriages failed because each time I married, I was *not ready to remarry and ended up marrying the wrong person for the wrong reasons.* I wondered, *Am I alone in this?* I began asking other redivorced people what had happened to them. Most I spoke with agreed with me on two things: They married before they should have and for the wrong reasons. They, too, suffered the consequences.

Today, I know a great deal about marriage and divorce. I've spent some years counseling divorced people and researching their behavior. I teach with Jim Smoke, my coauthor for this book, in our well-known divorce recovery program in California. I spend my days studying divorce. In our divorce recovery program, we have many participants who are redivorced. I have interviewed more than 100 such people. To develop a broader base of statistics on the subject, I employed a professional research company to help me conduct a national survey of 500 divorced and redivorced people. Questions I asked included: What were your reasons for remarrying? What were your circumstances at the time you remarried? What's your remarriage and divorce story? Using this information, I was able to confirm why so many remarriages end in divorce: Many people—perhaps most—were not ready to remarry. As a result, they married the wrong person for the wrong reasons.

I came across some very telling stories, and, amazingly, the people

I interviewed were eager to describe what had happened to them. Many of their stories and comments appear in this book. You'll glean a lot from their insights. These divorced people were just like me; they wanted to tell what went wrong. When each person got a divorce, whether it was his (or her) first or a subsequent one, that individual was angry, bitter, and resentful. He blamed the other person and had trouble identifying what had really happened. After some time passed, though, this person was able to gain greater clarity about what went wrong, about the role he played, and the circumstances that led to the failed remarriage. He finally had time to reflect and separate facts from emotions. Now, each time someone tells me a story of a marriage that occurred even when there were obvious red flags, I want to ask, "Why would you marry under those circumstances?" But I don't ask because I know the answer, and so do you. Once you're in the throes of a relationship, logic goes out the window and you only see what you want to see. That's why if you want to do any better, you must look at this subject with a hard, cold eye *before* you get too deep into a relationship. Otherwise, you'll soon be so emotionally involved, you'll be unwilling to face the facts.

In my interviews, the same wrong reasons for remarrying kept resurfacing until I was able to consolidate them into 13 reasons for remarriage that are wrong. When you are not ready to remarry, but do so anyway for the wrong reasons, your chance of failure increases exponentially. It stands to reason, then, that if we can identify the circumstances that prevent us from being truly ready to remarry and recognize these faulty reasons ahead of time, we can avoid making these mistakes.

Let me help you avoid the marriage mistakes that result in divorce and explore what you can do to help your next marriage be a success.

Jim's Story

While Ed learned about divorce the hard way, I became an expert unintentionally. While working as a pastor of singles at Crystal Cathedral (then Garden Grove Community Church) in the mid

1970s, I found many of my singles struggling with the aftermath of divorce. As a result, I instituted a program I called divorce recovery. At that time there were few articles or books written on the subject. I had to be a pioneer and develop tools to help these divorced people. I launched the first national singles magazine, *Solo*. When I moved to work in Tempe, Arizona, I founded the Center for Divorce Recovery. All of this led to my first book, published by Harvest House in 1976, *Growing Through Divorce*. This book has helped more than 600,000 people recover from their divorce experience. Since that time, I have conducted over 700 workshops on divorce recovery and written 17 other books on the subject.

Unfortunately, one thing I have seen over and over is people not willing to put in the time and effort to *grow* through their divorce. Instead, they remarry for all the wrong reasons. Inevitably, these remarriages fail and the sufferers have to learn the same lessons again. When you're feeling desperate or frustrated with your current life as a single person, you are vulnerable to do something not in your best interest. One of my ten commandments for newly divorced people is, "Thou shall not try to reconcile thy past and reconstruct thy future by a quick, new marriage." In my book *Seven Keys to a Healthy Blended Family*, I point out that a remarriage is not simply a union of two people the way it was the first time. You will face new challenges with children—yours and those of your new spouse—and you will face all the problems your new spouse has as well as your own. You may even have to deal with your spouse's ex and his or her family. Is it any wonder then that you need to allow time to heal and to clearly understand the mistakes divorced people make to avoid stumbling into another marriage?

Divorce leaves a big void, and there is a strong temptation to fill the void through remarriage. In my 30-plus years of divorce counseling, I have seen thousands of desperate people who wanted someone else to fix their problems. While some were so frozen they went into perpetual mourning and hid out in a self-made cocoon, others were immediately ready to move on. They came to our divorce recovery workshops to find their next mate. Neither approach leads to a healthy recovery. It's important not to drag your unresolved baggage into a remarriage. The only way to avoid doing this is to invest enough time in your recovery and be on guard for the traps we outline in this book.

Finding the right one to remarry can lead to a lifetime of fulfillment. Choosing the wrong one will lead to inevitable pain and likely another agonizing divorce.

You Can Do Better

We are not the first to observe that divorce is often caused by people choosing the wrong one for the wrong reasons. A few well-known Christian psychologists have noticed this fact. Dr. Phil McGraw, in his book *Relationship Rescue,* says:

> Research shows that over two-thirds of couples, married or otherwise, who attend relationship counseling are worse or at least no better after one year. The divorce rate in America refuses to drop below fifty percent and twenty percent of us will divorce not once but twice in our lifetime....No one ever taught you how to select a good mate....As a result, you probably chose your mate for the wrong reasons.[1]

Dr. Neil Clark Warren of eHarmony.com, who has counseled many couples, said in his book *Falling in Love for All the Right Reasons:*

> Many people will marry and divorce several times in their search for a truly satisfying relationship....The more I studied the matter, the more convinced I became that the overwhelming majority of failed marriages I encountered were in trouble on the day of the wedding. Quite simply, one or both members of the couple had chosen the wrong person to marry.[2]

You don't have to make the mistakes these counselors mention. We will show you how to avoid them. You *can* make some progress if you study the wrong reasons detailed in this book and work on understanding your motives for wanting to remarry *before* you're in the trenches with someone new. The truth is, the "bad reasons" aren't terribly fantastical or staggering in their shock value. But they are prevalent, and many of these will resonate with you if you're divorced.

Let the statistics alone be enough to convince you that you need to ratchet up your "remarriage IQ." Consider that in our national survey of 500 redivorced people, a whopping 88 percent said they married the wrong person for one or more of the 13 wrong reasons we discuss in this book.

Basically, the only person reading this book who gets a free pass to ignore all the relevant and compelling evidence we present is someone who has never been divorced or never wants to marry again. And our guess is that you wouldn't be reading *Finding the Right One After Divorce* if you fell into one of those categories. Once we reveal the wrong reasons, we will take a look at the flip side—the optimistic, bright platform that is filled with the *right reasons* to remarry. What conditions should be in place before you remarry to put the odds of success in your favor? How will you know you are ready to remarry? That's what divorced people need to know. Then you will be able to find the *right one* to marry.

Our hope is that you will use the information provided here to evaluate your own situation. We suggest you take the Ready2Remarry Test at the end of this book to achieve some important goals. Find out if you're in a good place to walk down that aisle one more time. Get briefed on the wrong reasons for remarrying. Assess whether you're remarrying for healthy reasons (same for your fiancé). Evaluate whether you have found the right one. Avoid becoming a divorceaholic.

Among the many nuggets of wisdom in *Finding the Right One After Divorce,* you'll be helped as you…

• face the fact that divorce creates emotional, physical, and financial circumstances that cause you to be vulnerable and not ready for remarriage.

- gain an understanding of the wrong reasons that people remarry.

- broaden your perspective by reading marriage anecdotes in which many people tell how and why they remarried the wrong person for the wrong reasons when they were yet unhealed from their divorces.

- learn to recognize the signals of marrying for the wrong reasons.

- get tips on ways to deal with your problems that can trigger a wrong remarriage.

- receive a plan for healing from divorce that will help you avoid making remarriage mistakes.

- take a test to gauge your remarriage readiness.

- review the right reasons that help you find the right one for you.

- examine some remarriage stoppers that may be holding you back even when you are ready to remarry.

- learn about some remarriage myths and gain reassurance that you are not alone in dealing with marriage, divorce, remarriage, and redivorce.

- learn what it takes to find the right one.

- lower your odds of another divorce.

Certainly, it's no secret that Americans have trouble with marriage. Lots of us are repeat offenders who are led down the gnarly paths of family breakups, pain and suffering, and children caught in divorce crossfire. Though bookstores are now filled with books on marriage, divorce, and remarriage, you will find precious little that has been written about the *reasons* why so many remarriages fail and what you can do to avoid that outcome. We strongly believe in marriage. In fact, one reason for writing this book is to share what we have learned so you can benefit from our knowledge and the experiences of other people who remarried before they were ready. If you follow the advice in this book and avoid the 13 mistakes, you will have a much better chance of finding the right one for a happy and successful remarriage. And that's a wonderful thing.

Make yourself marriage-worthy by making better choices, and you'll be glad you took the time to change your mate-selection tactics. Positively, absolutely. We all fear change, but sometimes that's exactly what it takes to be successful in those life skills in which we're not naturals. It's okay to admit you're marriage-challenged. It happens. You can live with it. What's not okay is to keep repeating the same costly mistakes.

Yes, Ed is a recovered divorceaholic who is now reveling in the joys of a great marriage. And my (Jim) marriage is very happy and secure. We can help you achieve the same thing. We want you to know when not to consider remarriage. We'll share the tools to help you heal and grow so you will become ready. Of course, we can't guarantee 100 percent that your next marriage will be successful, but we can give you time-proven, biblically based wisdom that will guide you in your recovery and provide insights about what to look for in a potential mate. You can script yourself a rosier future and reap the rewards of better choices that will lead to a great marriage.

1
The Greatest Problem from Divorce

❧ ❧ ❧

Marriage is the triumph of imagination
over intelligence.

Second marriage is the triumph of hope
over experience.

What is it about Americans and marriage? National statistics on divorce in this country are alarming. Remarriages are so common that they account for half of all marriages. This truly translates to a national epidemic when we consider that so many divorced people are repeat offenders whose actions wreak havoc and create family fissures, individual suffering, and loss of self-esteem. Yet few address *why* this is happening or how to avoid it.

Not Again

You probably know from personal experience how painful and disheartening divorce can be. In our divorce recovery workshops, we hear every story imaginable. It is incredibly sad to hear of so many broken dreams, so much agony from confused children, and so much anger, resentment, and confusion from the parents. No other event in human existence except death is so tormenting and life changing. People sob, they rant, they blame, they plead, they scream, and, underneath, they horribly hurt. We do everything we can to try to calm them and reassure them that, in time, they will heal and life will become more normal again.

But one thing upsets us more than the immediate agony we observe in divorced people. We tell them this unsettling thought: The greatest problem from divorce is *not* what you think. You may feel like you will never be the same. You are in intense pain. You can't imagine that the heartache will ever go away. You have a kaleidoscope of emotions ranging from shock, sadness, anger, bitterness, helplessness, hopelessness, guilt, shame, stress, insecurity, low self-esteem, to loneliness—and that's just on the first day. Then you are confronted with the seemingly insurmountable task of readjusting your life to a whole new reality. You have new financial strains, challenges with your children, even legal issues to resolve. *What could be worse than all of this?* you ask. We know for sure that in time you will recover. Those of us who have gone through divorce, or observed others who have, know that most of these consequences are short term, although the healing process takes time and effort. Just ask most people who have been divorced for more than five years. They will tell you it wasn't easy, but they are okay now. They have adjusted.

But that one thing we mentioned that upsets us more than seeing the trauma divorced people go through is *the* greatest problem from divorce. We know that almost half of these people who choose to remarry will go through divorce again.

The Trauma of Repeat

Some people say that a repeat divorce is easier than the first one. Total baloney. Anyone who has been through multiple divorces will tell you it doesn't get any easier the next time. What do we feel?

Shattered Self-Esteem

You think you have low self-esteem after the first divorce? Imagine how you would feel after the second or third? You have lost all self-confidence. If you thought maybe the first divorce was a fluke, now you're not so sure. If you thought your ex was all to blame, now you see that you are the common denominator in these divorces. If you think friends and family had a high regard for your character, you wonder what they are thinking now.

Something's Wrong with You

Now you begin to think there really is something wrong with you. Your self-perception as a mature, rational individual goes out the window. If you felt like a loser after the first divorce, you get strong confirmation after a repeat.

Fear of Remarriage

The more times you are divorced, the more you fear trying it again. Do you want to risk that trauma all over again? Can you take another failed marriage? Can you subject your children to another broken home? Are you willing to go through the agony and cost of another breakup? Are you ready to chance that all those plans and dreams you have could go up in smoke again? A number of the people in our national survey said that after a few attempts, they were through. They wanted no part of marriage. It became too difficult, too complicated, too risky.

Why Do People Have Failed Remarriages?

Today, much has been written about divorce, divorce recovery, life after divorce, dating, remarriage, blended families, and the like. Little has been written about why so many *remarriages* fail. Before discussing our findings in more detail, we want to expose you to some theories about why those who divorce have "a not much better than even" chance of making it the next time. In general, these reasons are best summarized as divorce due to marrying people who have debilitating deficits.

Baggage Handlers

There are many theories implied in common folklore about why some people have repeat divorces. One of these is "baggage." It's true.

If you are divorced, you have heaps of baggage. You have emotional scars—the hurts, wounds, anger, fears, hang-ups, and skepticisms of a failed marriage. Then there is the physical baggage—the children, the debts, the ongoing necessary connection with the ex-spouse. Some believe this baggage lessens your chance that a new marriage can succeed. There is some reality to this. If you enter a new marriage refusing to let go of the past or not allowing your new mate to be first, the marriage may falter from the start. But let's face it: Everyone has baggage. It just depends on how you handle it and what you do with it. Many second marriages do succeed even with baggage in tow. If you and your new spouse recognize the realities *before* the marriage and decide in advance how you will deal with all of it, the past won't be an insurmountable problem. Remember, more than half of remarriages are successful.

Bad Boys and Girls

When divorce attorneys ask their clients what led to the breakup of their marriages, addictions and other bad behaviors are mentioned in a list of the top ten. If a divorced person has a drinking or drug problem and isn't able to get this under control before his or her next marriage, is it any surprise that the second marriage will stumble? Other addictions such as gambling or sex likewise create risks to the repeat offender. Some people have spending or eating compulsions or similar hang-ups. If you have any of these types of problems that led to your divorce, you need to get clean and fixed before even considering remarriage. Telling the new fiancé the truth about your problem is also a must.

Needless to say, if you marry someone with such ongoing problems, you're being foolhardy.

Quitters

Another theory about why multiple divorces occur is that some people just can't stick with anything they do. They're quitters. This is the belief that there is a certain type of person who is quicker to quit than to tough it out. In contrast, it's believed people who marry and never divorce are more committed to the institution of marriage or to their spouse, or both. Another version of this theory is that the hurt and cynical attitude created by the first divorce makes you less likely to stay in a marriage given the eventual ups and downs. It goes like this: After seeing that you survived the first divorce (and you're already branded a divorced person), it's easier to bail out the next time. If your next marriage is difficult, you may feel it's easier to divorce again because you know you will recover. Reality check: While it may be true that divorce is less scary the second time because you know what to expect, who wants to go through that entire trauma again?

Failure-Prone People

The premise here is that those who divorce multiple times tend to be failures in many other facets of life. Are divorced people just losers? This theory can't fly since 50 percent of marriages end in divorce. There aren't that many losers in the world! Still, anyone who has been involved in the dating scene can probably confirm that there are a few out there.

The Real Reasons for Divorce

Our research tells us that these reasons—baggage, addictions, hang-ups, quitter-types, and the failure-prone—are not the major reasons for so many multiple divorces. No doubt some remarriages fail because of these various reasons. Some people probably are not the marrying type, and they won't stick it out through the ups and downs. Then there are the complexities of remarriage with children where blood is thicker than water. If the kids, even adult children, pose a problem, some parents may choose them instead of the new spouse. Financial issues also add a layer of difficulty to a remarriage. When people get married the first time, few have any possessions. In contrast, people in their 40s, 50s, or 60s have a lot. They feel the need to protect their money because they do not have time to earn it all over again.

No, the answer for why most subsequent marriages fail is that divorce creates circumstances that cloud our judgment and may lead us to remarry before we are ready, and we may do so for the wrong reasons. We may even choose one of the four "ill-equipped for marriage" types just mentioned as our next spouses. When we are still adrift in blame-shifting, stigma-fighting, and emotion-sorting, we do not make great mates—and we are not in a good position to select one. Unfortunately, we forget that having gone through a divorce means we need to take some time to reempower ourselves. And what we do not need to do is plunge forward mindlessly into dating, mating, and another marriage.

Many a divorced person does not have a clue what went wrong the last time he (or she) recited vows, but he doesn't let that keep him from lining up at the matrimonial scrimmage line for another shot at the end-zone. The marriage-challenged have a hard time seeing the truth. They thrive on love, courtship, romance. They want someone to fix their problems. They quickly end up married again. Bottom line, if you go forward with remarrying when you are still just as clueless as you were the last time you chose a mate, you are very likely to make another marriage mistake—the last thing you want to happen. If you seem to be drawn to remarry impulsively, no matter how prudent you are in other aspects of living, hopefully this book will help you hold off.

Two Types of Remarriages

Not all redivorces involve marrying the wrong person for the wrong reasons. Some remarriages that end in divorce were not due to bad choices. A woman in our divorce recovery workshop said she was happily remarried for more than 30 years, had four beautiful children, but then her husband had a heart attack. This event pushed him over the edge, and he left her to pursue a new life. Clearly this was not a failed remarriage on her part.

If a remarriage ends within three to ten years, this is generally a sign of marrying the wrong person for the wrong reasons. A recent study reveals that among all remarriages, 25 percent end in divorce or separation within the first five years and 40 percent within ten years. There is ample evidence that many remarriages occur because people were not ready to remarry, resulting in finding the wrong person from the start.

2

Post-Divorce Syndrome

❧ ❧ ❧

Men marry because they are tired,
women because they are curious;
both are disappointed.

OSCAR WILDE

Maybe it's not a disease, but it sure is a psychological upheaval and an undesirable condition. After getting a divorce, people face circumstances that produce a large number of emotions, feelings, and responses that disable their abilities to function as they would in more normal circumstances. We call this set of things that people deal with after divorce the Post-Divorce Syndrome.

The important point about this syndrome is that it heightens your vulnerability to act in ways that are often not in your best interest. Let's review some of these symptoms so that you can better understand what this syndrome is about, recognize when you have this condition, and know how to deal with it.

Denial

Many divorced people remain in denial that this is happening to them. We have seen people reject that a divorce is imminent until the time the final papers are handed to them. "This isn't happening.

He will change his mind. Something will happen and this will all go away." A sign of this is when you refuse to use the word "divorce." You use terms like separated, moved out, and thinking it over. When denial is extreme, you act like the marriage never happened. One person in our divorce recovery group said he grieved for a few days and that was it. If you don't acknowledge what is happening, grieve, and go through the steps to recovery, you may jump into another marriage with all your bad baggage intact, having learned nothing from the divorce. If you don't deal with it sooner, you will later…usually during the next marriage.

Shock

Whether you are the one who leaves or the one who was left, there is a degree of shock when a divorce occurs. Reality hits you like a ton of bricks. You can't function. You are incapable of thinking or doing. This generally lasts a short period of time for most people. But if you seem stuck in that mode, you need to get counseling so you can move forward.

Shame

Divorce, for some, is the ultimate sin. To you being divorced means you are a failure, a loser, a sinner. You have just joined the ranks of a club of people that includes drunks, drug addicts, thieves, and so forth. You are no better than a common criminal or a person from the other side of the tracks. You may take divorce so hard that you cannot face your family and friends. It doesn't matter whether you cheated on your spouse or he cheated on you or any other situation. You wear the scarlet letter of divorce, and it will always be imprinted on your chest. You are branded for life. Sadly, some churches treat you this way, too. Rather than displaying love and compassion, they look upon you as a leper or a second-class citizen.

Guilt

Somewhat related to shame is guilt. People who get divorced often have bundles of guilt. It shows up in the "if onlys." "If only

I had been a better cook, housekeeper, breadwinner, lover, parent, then he (or she) would not have left." People who leave have guilt. "She counted on me. I said until death do us part. How will she get along now? I have hurt her deeply." It goes on and on—the guilt you feel when a marriage ends. How can you alleviate the guilt? You may try to stay connected to your ex, which only makes matters worse. You may focus on all the awful things your ex did in order to justify your own behavior.

Sadness

Divorce is an ending of a shared dream. How can this be anything other than a sad situation? No matter how relieved you are to extricate yourself from an intolerable situation, there is still the memory of positive expectations of what was to be. God can help you heal this sadness. However, for some divorced people, they forget all the Bible teaches and their sadness turns into something worse, such as bitterness or hopelessness.

Anger/Bitterness/Resentment

If the marriage died long before the decision was made to divorce, there may be little anger or negative feelings. Or if both parties want the divorce, then there may be relief without much anger on both sides. For most divorced people, however, there are significant recriminations. If one party left the other for someone else, then resentments are likely to be strong. It's easier when you can blame the other person. Even when you were the one leaving, you can be resentful about what your ex did to drive you away. This original anger can turn into a long-lasting "root of bitterness" that can eat you up. You are bitter at your ex. You are bitter about your marriage and divorce. You are bitter at the world. You are not in a good state of mind to be reconsidering remarriage.

Low Self-Esteem

This is one of the toughest problems caused by divorce. With all the blaming of yourself and your ex that goes on, it's difficult to maintain your sense of worth. "She left me for some guy who couldn't even keep a job." "His affair with that cheap secretary was a slap in the face." As the song says, there are 50 ways to leave your lover—and some of them can really damage you or your ex. Nothing much can be said in the way of an apology that will fix the pain. Most people recover from this ego-blow by eventually seeing that they have value and that other people do want them. The risk is that you try to make this happen too quickly. It's the old story of going out to quickly find another person to prove to yourself and your ex that you are desirable. This exaggerates the problem.

Stress

The social readjustment rating scale by Holmes-Rahe lists a variety of life events and their level of difficulty in terms of our ability to adjust to them. Not surprisingly, the death of a spouse is at the top of the list. But second is divorce—above jail time, death of a close family member, and personal injury. Yes, adjustment to divorce is *tough*. It's not surprising then that this event causes tremendous stress. You are now alone in the world. You have responsibilities that now fall only on you. Friends are taking sides. Bills have to be paid by you. You're living these problems now. These stresses can drive you to distraction. They can drive you to want an instant spouse replacement, too.

Insecurity

All the problems people are left with in divorce cause massive insecurity. How will you take care of the kids on your own? How will you pay the mortgage? How will you deal with your emotional ups and downs and those of your children? Will your ex let you visit the kids without a fight? You face the emotional and financial insecurity of a totally new situation without any experience to know how it will play out. You're on uncharted ground without a road map. You are bound to be insecure for a time.

Helplessness

Some people get right to taking care of everything. They are make-it-happen types. Others, however, may have relied too much on the ex. Now you have to cook or repair things around the house or take care of the car. You may feel a sense of panic and complete helplessness. This situation can put you in a tough spot. Either you take charge and learn to do things yourself, get help from friends, or find someone, such as a new spouse, to rescue you—a bad option.

Hopelessness

When it's all too much and overpowering, you may develop a feeling of hopelessness. The fear of the future is paralyzing. "Why bother." "My life is over." "Everything is downhill from here." "Nothing will ever be the same for me." "Even time won't fix the mess I'm in." "No one cares." This hopeless feeling is very common in divorced people. Don't panic if you feel this way. It will pass. But don't try to fix it with someone else.

Loneliness

Last, but not least, is the reality of being and feeling alone. After the relief wears off that the divorce is final, it's just you in this big house or new apartment. The screaming kids make it harder. There's no one to listen to you, no one to hug you, and no one to give you adult love. Those of us who have gone through divorce know exactly how this feels. It's an empty feeling tinged with a fear that it will always be this way…or at least for a long while.

What Now?

Okay, remember the reality of the situation. The vast majority of divorced people remarry—80 percent. Those of us who have already gone through the trauma *know* you can make it to the other side and have a wonderful life again *if*—notice that very big if—*if* you don't let the Post-Divorce Syndrome lead you to jump into another marriage before you are ready, before you "get whole."

Experts give this advice to people who have lost a spouse due to death: Don't make any big decisions. Don't sell the house. Don't move away. Don't do anything until at least a year has passed. They give this advice because they know that significant decisions that require rational, clear thinking cannot be made when you are in an emotional state. The same goes for divorce. Look at all the emotional upheaval that occurs in divorce and ask yourself, Can I make a life-altering decision like remarrying in this mental condition? The answer is, *No!* It usually takes at least two years to heal sufficiently to come out of the Post-Divorce Syndrome; longer for some people. Don't rush it.

While this is not a book about divorce recovery, chapter 19 outlines some of what has to happen for you to heal from this syndrome and become sufficiently independent to avoid remarrying for the wrong reasons. For more information, get Jim's book *Growing Through Divorce*.

3

Choosing
the Wrong One

❧ ❧ ❧

I was married by a judge.
I should have asked for a jury.

GROUCHO MARX

People in divorce recovery often ask us, "Why do remarriages fail?" It's a good question. The problem is that we can't enumerate the vast number of possible reasons. So how can this book provide any guidance about remarriage if there are so many reasons remarriages fail? Let us offer an unusual analogy.

Getting the Odds in Your Favor

In Ed's business career, he was an industry consultant. "I assisted companies in developing new products that today generate hundreds of millions of dollars in sales. When clients asked me, 'What are the reasons that new products fail?' I told them that there are hundreds of reasons. Products fail because they don't work, they taste bad, they break, they look awful, they're priced too high, they're not available where customers want them, they filled no customer need, they were inferior to competition, they were poorly advertised, and so forth." If there are that many reasons for failure, how can we ever hope to increase the odds of success beyond just chance? The answer is that there are strategic factors that, if ignored, will almost assure us of having a failure. In other words, if we launch a product breaking these rules, we almost guarantee that the new product will fail. From the start it will be "dead on arrival"—DOA. These strategic insights about the requirements for a successful new product were determined by studying successes as well as failures. So if we follow these strategies, we don't eliminate the possibility of failure because we can always mess up the execution, but we do *increase the odds of success.*

That's the way it is with remarriages. We have learned by studying successful remarriages and failures that if you remarry when you're not ready and for the wrong reasons, the marriage is likely to be DOA. Right from the start, you are on a path to failure because you made a poor choice for yourself. The marriage might succeed, but the odds are not good. Just like launching new products, you want to act when the odds are in your favor. Marrying for the right reasons doesn't guarantee a successful marriage because one party can still lose his balance and foul it up. He might change or have a midlife crisis. She might have an affair, go berserk, whatever—even 35 years after the wedding day. Understanding the right and wrong reasons and circumstances for remarriage increases the odds that your next marriage will be successful. The key is being ready to remarry so that you will make better choices finding the right one.

Failed Marriages: Bad Behaviors or Bad Choices?

When marriage counselors and other therapist types treat people in the throes of a collapsing marriage, they focus on a variety of issues they assume are the causes of the disharmony:

- deficient interpersonal skills
- poor communication

- unwillingness to compromise
- inability to control anger and temper
- lack of skill in conflict resolution
- lack of respect for the other person
- imbalance in the tasks performed by each partner
- bad habits or addictions
- not meeting needs
- blah, blah, blah

Many marriages do fail because one party or both have these problems. But another theory that explains many divorces is simply that someone made a bad choice from the start. Obviously, you are not well suited to be married to just anyone. Of the six-and-a-half-billion people in the world, there are probably a few thousand you could choose to whom you would be happily married. The rest would be bad choices for you. Also, there are many prospects out there that already have bad traits, addictions, and similar problems. Choose one of them, and you get a "divorce waiting to happen." Or if you have any of these unresolved issues yourself, you need to work on them before subjecting someone else to your problems.

Why Do We Make Poor Choices?

Marriage is one of the most important choices you will ever make. Our research reveals that many divorces occur simply because you or your spouse made a bad choice. Hence the marriage was DOA. No one deliberately makes poor choices. People get caught up in the experience and their decision-making suffers.

Suppose we take a less serious subject, but still an important one—buying a new car. You just bought the new Hyper-Turbo V-8, and now you are beginning to live with your decision. You are not too happy. In fact, you have serious buyer's remorse. You know you made a poor choice for yourself, and you wonder what happened that led to this unpleasant outcome. Here are some of the possibilities.

You ignored obvious negative information. You commute to work 150 miles a day, and gas prices have skyrocketed. The window sticker on this car said it only gets 8 miles per gallon. You knew this but decided at the time to overlook this fact. You were so enamored with this exciting vehicle that you minimized the importance of gas mileage when you signed those papers financing this honey.

You didn't ask the right questions. The salesperson would have told you that tires on this performance model only last 10,000 miles, but you never asked. You were in such a hurry to get that machine out on the road you failed to ask pertinent questions.

You didn't spend enough time or effort to get the information you should have. Your close friend just told you that this model has the lowest reliability rating by *Customer Reports.* They rated the car as having the poorest repair record of any model they ever tested. *Duh!* Why didn't you look into this before making the purchase?

You were tricked or deceived. The dealership where you purchased this Hyper-Turbo V-8 is not planning to carry that line of cars anymore, so they won't have a service facility to take care of any problems. Somehow they failed to mention this. You know you were tricked into buying this turkey. If they hadn't deceived you, you would have never considered this car.

Someone pressured you. Friends kept telling you that you would be swarmed with people to date if you were driving a Hyper-Turbo V-8. One friend said you would be a fool to get anything else. The salesperson concurred. He told you they had a sale on that was good only for the next ten minutes. If you didn't commit to this beauty now, she would cost thousands more tomorrow and maybe even be sold to some other lucky buyer.

You made up your mind ahead of time. When you went to the dealer, you were already convinced this was the car for you. No amount of conflicting or negative information would change your mind. You had a "Don't confuse me with the facts" mentality. You had made a decision, and nothing could divert you from your plan to purchase this model.

You didn't really know what you wanted. If you had taken the time to analyze what you needed in a new car, you would have concluded that the most important attributes it should have would be high gas mileage, room for five people (you commute with others), automatic transmission, and a low price to accommodate low monthly payments. Because you never spent the effort to analyze your needs, you ended up with the Hyper-Turbo V-8—a two-seat sports car with a 6-speed manual transmission, and a high-horsepower, gas-eating V-8 that costs twice what you can afford.

You were mesmerized. It was love at first sight. When you saw this car, its beauty was overwhelming. You were so taken by the appearance of this vehicle that you knew you had to have it. You were swept off your feet by this machine. Your friends would all be envious when you pulled up with this gorgeous hunk. You focused only on this one feature and ignored how the car fared on the other factors.

You were not thinking straight. Unfortunately, your old car blew up yesterday. You were stressed by all the problems you had with that piece of junk. It was always in the shop, dollaring you to death. You had just cancelled your insurance, so you got nothing when it disintegrated. Your boss told you to get some transportation and not to miss any more days of work. So you had to get wheels right away. You couldn't think straight with all that you were going through, so you grabbed the first thing the dealer showed you—the Hyper-Turbo V-8.

I'm sure you can relate to these scenarios. And many of the wrong reasons people remarry parallel these types of mistakes.

Test Yourself

We like practical subjects. We want this topic of remarriage to be practical for you. The only way that can happen is if you have tools to use to apply to your own situation so you can analyze whether you are ready to remarry, and whether your reasons are sound. To this end, we have prepared a Ready2Remarry Test presented at the end of this book to help you evaluate your circumstances and those of your prospective marriage partner.

Note: It only takes one person in a marriage to bring about a divorce. If your intended spouse is getting married for the wrong reasons, you may pay the price when he or she implodes. It takes two healthy people to have a healthy marriage. So as you read this book, think not just about yourself in these situations and circumstances, but also evaluate the person you are considering marrying.

To help you better relate to these issues, you might ask friends who have had multiple marriages what their circumstances were when they got married. Were they emotionally healthy enough to remarry? Did they remarry for what turned out to be wrong reasons? Don't ask why their marriages failed. You will get things like, "She had an affair." "He began ignoring me." These "end-of-story sagas" may be the final result of remarrying for the wrong reasons—the symptoms, not the causes.

Causes or Symptoms

When we talk to people about the concepts of "finding the right one," "ready to remarry," and "wrong reasons," we are often asked why psychotherapists and marriage counselors haven't focused on these issues. We have an answer: They solve problems. You go to a counselor when you're in a crisis. "My marriage is in trouble. Can you help me save it?" "I am getting a divorce. I am depressed. Can you help me get through it?" Who goes to a therapist when they are happy? Who calls a counselor when they have met someone and are excitedly considering marriage? Psychologists and psychiatrists see and treat the symptoms of bad choices already made.

Don't assume that marriage experts can fix the problems you create for yourself. The time to stop a DOA remarriage is *before* you say "I do."

4

Blind Spots
and Pressures

ઢ ઢ ઢ

One woman said to another,
"Aren't you wearing your wedding ring
on the wrong finger?"

The other replied, "Yes, I am.
I married the wrong man."

You picked up this book because you want us to help you understand how to find the right one to remarry, but you also want us to tell you how to guard against embarking on another marriage that won't work out. Anyone knows that once you become emotionally involved with someone, you can manufacture a multitude of rationalizations to keep the relationship going, no matter how much evidence that it is ill-fated. But you can indeed tip the odds in your favor for a successful remarriage if you gain clarity on the relationship *before* you find yourself emotionally entangled with another person. Try to stack up some relationship "credentials" before you leap into another marriage.

Love Isn't the Only Reason

Why do people marry? We are not talking about why you would select Mr. or Ms. Right. We are talking about why you would make the decision to "go to the chapel" with him or her. We marry because we are in love with another person, right? Love is the emotional glue that is so important for making a marriage work. But love is not the only reason—and sometimes not the primary reason—people exchange rings. Maybe being in love is a necessary condition before you'll say "I do." But just because you fall in love with someone doesn't mean you should decide to get married.

The motivation to marry is based on a variety of factors that relate to fulfilling personal wants and needs. Sometimes these are healthy needs, sometimes not. To help you see more clearly what we are talking about, look at why many young first-timers marry. They do so to escape from parents or to please them, to legitimize having sex, to feel grown-up, to avoid being left out, to have children, and so on. Almost any potential spouse could fill those needs, and therein lies the problem.

If you are divorced, you know that love does not conquer all. The "more rational" reasons for marrying are critical to understand, especially for remarriages. After divorce, you have a whole new set of circumstances versus when you got married the first time. You're smarter. You now know what marriage is all about. But with all the positives, come other circumstances that can create blind spots and pressures that you didn't have when you were younger.

Blind Spots

The reason remarriage is so difficult is that it follows divorce, a painful event that creates a wide range of problems for everyone. The Post-Divorce Syndrome is alive and well. An important challenge for you is getting centered before you marry again. But you face roadblocks to doing that, not the least of which are the numbing, debilitating pain and sense of hopelessness that divorce creates. Then there are the real-world problems, too. When divorce occurs, both parties are usually worse off. You need two homes, two cars, two of most everything. And divorce itself can be costly with legal fees. Then there are the children. You suddenly have responsibilities that were previously shared. Remarriage requires finding an adult who can act as a parent without actually being the father or mother. It also means that you are not only marrying your intended spouse, but his or her children, family, and maybe even ex-spouse. This requires maturity and responsibility. In effect, people considering remarriage should be a lot more practical in deciding to remarry and in choosing a mate. But the reverse can happen if you can't manage on your own. Becoming single after 5, 10, or 50 years of marriage is tough. Everybody was dating when you first got married. No one you know is now. Now you're single, but all your friends are married. You have to adjust to being single in what for you is a "married person's world." Remarrying with these pressures can lead you to compromise, to settle, to overlook things.

When we ask people why they divorced, why their marriages failed, most blame the other person. They say it was because the ex had bad traits or habits: "Will had a drinking problem," "Kelly couldn't control her spending," "Harvey was always at the office," "Alison took drugs," and "Jacob chased women." The critical question is why did you choose to marry him or her in the first place? Even if all those bad things were true, why blame your ex for your choices? And when we ask if there were any clues that these patterns existed prior to the marriage, many admit that the behaviors were already there to some degree. Some knew their spouses had the same pattern in their previous marriage. "My wife told me her former husband left her because she was so moody." "I knew my husband had cheated on his first wife, too."

Others say they never saw these bad behaviors, but they also confided they dated for six months or less.

We bear some responsibility for our failed marriages if we don't allow sufficient time to get to know the other person or if we choose to ignore warning signs when they appear. Our belief is that most people are sane; they know what is in their best interest. They *can* choose wisely when right circumstances prevail. This caveat—right circumstances—is often the problem in marriage and remarriage decisions.

Dumb Mistakes Others Make

You can probably call it correctly for others almost every time when you see them make irrational decisions about marriage. Think about the friend you knew who made plans to remarry when everyone was talking about what a huge mistake she was making. You knew the boyfriend would be unfaithful. He was flirting with you even at the wedding. But she wouldn't listen; she would hear none of it. Or remember the poor guy who married "Hostile Harriet," as you used to call her. You knew he wouldn't last six months with her. Why is it so much easier to see others' mistakes rather than our own? You can even understand your own misled motivations to marry, but usually when you're looking back five to ten years after the fact and have the benefit of 20/20 hindsight. Many people present clear pictures of mistakes they've made in marriage and remarriage with the advantage of a perspective gained from the years following divorce. But when you're in the glow of a new relationship, you have a great deal more trouble getting a handle on your own motivation to remarry and finding a way to act in your own best interest.

You Can Do Better

We know you can do better next time if you will take the time to understand why so many remarriages are DOA. They're doomed because we remarry the wrong person for the wrong reasons. We do this because we find ourselves in circumstances that cause us to make bad choices. If you can understand these wrong reasons to remarry and allow yourself to grow and not succumb to them, you will make better choices and drastically increase the odds that the next marriage will succeed. On these pages, you can discover the most common "wrong reasons," ways to guard against them, and tips for getting to a place where you're not vulnerable to remarry in these circumstances. Then you will get a look at some of the right reasons. Using the advice offered and the tools provided, you will be in a position for finding the right one after divorce.

But let us give you a warning: Many of the people we interviewed who were redivorced told us that reading this book wouldn't have kept them from making the mistakes they did. It wouldn't have made a bit of difference. They would have just gone merrily right ahead believing they were ready to remarry and marrying the wrong person for the wrong reasons. They said probably nothing would have stopped them from their DOA remarriage. Reason? Once they were so emotionally involved with the other person, they would have provided themselves with all the rationalizations needed to keep the relationship going, no matter what brightly colored, billowing, red flags were raised. So here are some things you need to do to make sure you benefit from this book.

Learn before you get involved. Wrap your mind around the reasons you won't get married next time—the wrong motivations—*before* you get involved with your next partner. Don't allow yourself to get emotionally involved with a prospective remarriage candidate until you have sufficiently healed and understand fully the wrong reasons and the right ones. If you're the vulnerable type, don't date until you have thoroughly understood the prescriptions offered here and you're on a serious path to getting healed after your divorce.

Identify with people who did it wrong. Read about each of the 13 wrong reasons. Look at the comments of people who married for these reasons and see what has a familiar ring. You may think you'll feel a sting when that happens, but quite the contrary. Instead, there's a sense of comfort in finally coming to grips with why you're doing some illogical things—and putting a name on it. Then, when you have identified the kinds of mistakes you tend to make, you can take the necessary steps to solve your own problems rather than expecting a new marriage partner to do it for you.

Be on your guard and don't rationalize away concerns. Romance, sex, loneliness, and many other factors that draw people together are strong drivers that can be difficult to resist. You will have to be on guard consciously so that you can avoid remarrying when warning signs surface. Keep a running list of the good things about any prospective spouse and a list of the red flags. If any are major issues, give the relationship more time or back out. Keep remembering the stories of people in this book who paid a high price because they rushed into marriage or said yes when they knew they should have said no.

Know the right reasons to remarry. When you get to the chapter revealing the right reasons, make certain you understand them. Don't remarry until you know you are ready!

Test yourself. Continually use the Ready2Remarry Test to help you double-check if you're making progress and are ready to find your next (and final) mate.

Bottom line: None of this is easy, but if you read and follow the recommendations just mentioned, you will put the odds in your favor of finding the right one for you and having a successful remarriage.

We promised in this book to help direct you to find the right one to remarry. But you need to know that the reason so many don't find the right one is that they settle for the wrong one as a result of pressures that lead them to marry for the wrong reasons. So before telling you about the right reasons and how to choose wisely, we'll examine the 13 wrong reasons to remarry. As you read about each one, see if you personally identify with any of the people in these stories or have the problems they had. If you do, pay particular attention to the suggestions for how to avoid succumbing to these bad motives that usually lead to a remarriage mistake. Note the issues that made them *not* ready to remarry.

5

Wrong Reason #1
Rescue Me

❧ ❧ ❧

*A good marriage is at least 80 percent good
luck in finding the right person at the right
time. The rest is trust.*

NANETTE NEWMAN

We've seen the rescue theme repeatedly in our study of redivorced people. Of all the wrong reasons for remarriage, this is probably the most insidious simply because the desire to nurture/save/help is so intrinsic to the rescuer's persona. This means to change his stripes he must rescript his entire approach to the opposite sex. This is doable, sure, but not so easy. Read on and you'll see why.

Save Me

One of the most popular movie themes in our culture is the rescue. In the movie *Pretty Woman,* Richard Gere, playing a successful businessman, saves the good-hearted hooker Julia Roberts. In *An Officer and a Gentleman,* Richard Gere, this time a young military officer, whisks factory-worker Deborah Winger out of her drab, blue-collar, workaday existence. Granted, film audiences realize they're watching fantasy scenarios, but that doesn't lessen the appeal of seeing a Prince Charming swoop in to save a woman in jeopardy. The idea is always exciting. It resonates with people of all ages to an incredible degree. And it's also a classic because in real life these situations play out every day of the week. None makes front-page news or wins an Oscar, but men and women are busily rescuing each other rather routinely…or trying to anyway.

While rescue makes an intriguing plot line, in the real world it's a dangerous route to take. It's filled with land mines and potholes and all manner of disappointments. We want to believe that when two people become involved, they will marry and live happily ever after. Any time you see a person face obstacles that keep him from ending up with his perfect mate, you grieve for that individual. You want someone to help him fix his problems and deliver to him a better life. Isn't that what love should do? Well, actually, no. Love is not supposed to problem-solve or give you a person who can make you complete or issue you a one-way ticket out of loneliness, desperation, and drudgery. Love isn't really a caped crusader, a clever action hero, or a rehab expert. In the world of everyday marriage, where we happen to live, rescues rarely work out. Here are three very good reasons why.

Dissimilar circumstances. Remove the emotional veil and ask yourself in the bright light of day, using our movie models as an example, how could these relationships work? What's the likelihood of long-term success in a marriage of a prominent businessman and a prostitute or a military officer and a factory worker? When people join in marriage who have little in common or very different backgrounds or belief systems, the odds of success are diminished. What people have in common in this situation is that one needs help and the other offers to provide it, not a good, solid basis for any marriage. There are many ways to be "unequally yoked" in addition to religious beliefs.

Unequal partners. Another reason that rescues fail is inequality. These are relationships in which one person is dependent and the other is in control. One has all the power, and the other has little or none. This is not a marriage of equals or anything resembling a partnership. Marriage requires mutual respect, and in rescue setups, that's usually not the dynamic. One is superior, the other inferior because that's the seesaw holding the relationship together. A detour that may tip the scales adversely is a burgeoning independence in the rescued. When that happens via education, job training, or increased confidence, the rescued no longer needs the rescuer as much and may even resent the other's dominance. The rescued may eventually become independent and decide that she no longer has any reason to stay with the rescuer.

Loveless equation. If someone needs rescuing, any Spider Man will do. Love is not part of the equation. Yes, you may appreciate the heck out of your rescuer, but gratitude and love are not the same things. Both belong in marriage. Marriage without love rarely flourishes.

Gender-Neutral Rescues

Don't get the idea that we are talking only about men rescuing women. It also works the other way around. In the national survey Ed undertook, a number of women said they had rescued men and the resulting marriages had failed. Successful women sometimes look for less-successful men who aren't threatened by their status. Of course, you don't see this scenario in movies because viewers couldn't root for a female business mogul pursuing a perpetual loser in an attempt to salvage him. Observers would think she was crazy.

By the way, we are not saying that marriage partners always must be of equal social and economic status. But what we are suggesting is that if one person married another in order to pull off a rescue, both partners should consider the caveat "watch out what you wish for because you just might get it." The rescuer gets a codependent mate who's really not his type. The rescued gets an always-in-power savior whom she doesn't love. The reality of rescue: You have a rescuer and a rescuee, both of whom are marrying for the wrong reasons. So how do people take on these roles? And why do some divorced people want to rescue or be rescued?

Confused and Bemused

Most divorced people don't like where they are. They never thought they would find themselves divorced. Does anyone really want his or her marriage to end? Whether you're the person leaving or the one left behind, you didn't expect the marriage to end this way. This fact alone sets you up for rescue. You're a mess emotionally, even if you keep telling yourself that you're doing just fine. Although you may feel a profound sense of relief when your divorce is final because the fighting ends, that relief can very quickly turn to sorrow.

Divorced people go though a process similar to grieving a death. The late psychiatrist Elisabeth Kübler-Ross, a noted expert on how people respond to death, explained that when people know they are going to die, they first experience denial and isolation, then anger, next bargaining, followed by depression, and finally acceptance. After your divorce, you're likely on an emotional treadmill, constantly walking through grief, anger, resentment, bitterness, sorrow, hopelessness, fear—even simultaneously at times. Making matters worse is the fact that your social, economic, and family circumstances are turned upside down. Friends often take sides. Your finances are a mess no matter how much or how little money you have. If you have children, they are upset and depressed, sometimes showing regressive behaviors, especially if they are pawns in the power struggle. They naturally will be reeling from the conflict and confusion. Do these circumstances sound even slightly conducive to making a sound decision about selecting a marriage partner? Even if you wait a few years, your situation may still be subpar. No wonder you wind up in a post-divorce maelstrom of emotions and spending a lot of time daydreaming that someone will rescue you from the nightmare and repair your messed-up life. You, the potential rescuee, would love to have someone end your misery. A rescuee is coming from a position of neediness and insecurity.

On the other side, the one doing the rescue is also coming from an orbit of neediness and insecurity. We interviewed a number of men who sought out women to rescue. They did so because they, maybe unknowingly at the time, believed such women would be dependent on them. The rescuer has power; he is in control. He assumes the rescued person will be forever grateful, dependent, and won't leave him like the last wife did. Ah, but then that creepy thing called reality intrudes and bursts the rescuer's bubble. Rescue guy is disappointed when he discovers that he can't depend on the codependency lasting.

To show you how badly the whole rescue game can go, let's look at the lives of some rescuers and rescuees. And don't tell yourself, "Oh, that's not me. Those are extreme cases. I would never be that way." Rescue is just a matter of degree. You don't have to be poor or dysfunctional to be susceptible to a rescue. And you may not even be aware that you're a rescuer looking for someone to save. Try to be at your most introspective as you review the following examples of some very successful people who married for the wrong reasons.

A Second Chance to Have a First Marriage

Ken grew up in a middle-class family in the Midwest. He was a talented, smart boy who never lacked female companionship. In high school he was popular and dated a number of attractive girls. After high school he moved away to attend college in another state. During that time his father died, and his mother had to sell the family home. Ken began to feel insecure about his future.

After college, he returned to his hometown, where he came across a woman he'd dated in high school. She had just returned from traveling abroad. Like Ken, she was uncertain of the future. Both had a sense of aimlessness. After two months, they decided to get married. They identified with each other's circumstances and believed that marriage was the answer. But their bond unraveled quickly. The marriage was difficult, and three years into it, Ken's wife told him she'd met an actor and was moving in with him. Ken was devastated. He asked himself, *How could this happen to me? I am a failure. Who would ever want me again? I'm tainted as a loser.*

For the longest time, Ken was morose. He moped around. His friends didn't want to be around him. But worst of all, he wouldn't consider dating even after two years had passed since his divorce. He was so bitter and angry at his ex-wife that he thought he could never forgive her. She not only rejected him and left him, but she had also humiliated him by immediately moving in with someone else.

Six months later, Ken had a change of heart on the issue of dating when a friend mentioned that his girlfriend had a sister who needed an escort to a party. Sara was five years younger than Ken and had just finished college. She came from a very strict home where her father regulated her every move. As a result, Sara was somewhat naïve. She had dated guys her age in college, but none had shown any real interest in her. When Ken and Sara met, something happened instantly between them. They labeled it "love at first sight." In Ken, Sara saw a mature, older man who was more substantial than the boys her age. She liked that he seemed sophisticated and worldly like her father. And from Ken's perspective, Sara was a joy in that she was worlds removed from the jaded women he knew who were divorced and desperate. And, most important, he liked that she was so flipped over him. It was clear she would never leave him like his first wife.

The relationship seemed very promising. Then Ken decided he wanted to move to Nevada. Sara's father insisted that if she were to accompany him, she could only go as a married woman. Sara saw two great opportunities in getting married: a chance to escape the stranglehold her father had on her, and the start of a life with someone who seemed wonderful. What kept running through Ken's mind was that Sara would give him a second chance to have a first marriage. How excellent was that? *Surely,* he reasoned, *marrying her will wipe out the bad memory of my first marriage as if it never happened.*

So they did marry. Fast-forward three years. Nothing was what each partner expected. Ken turned out to be more like Sara's father than she thought—and not in a good way. He was controlling and domineering. Sara realized she had traded her overbearing dad for a new father figure who was equally difficult. She fought with Ken when he made suggestions. She found his attitude demeaning. On the flip side, Ken grew tired of Sara because her naiveté began to bore him. At social functions, he was almost ashamed of her because she acted childlike. Furthermore, he didn't feel inclined to confide in her because he didn't respect her. As pressures continued to mount, they grew apart.

Complicating the situation further was Ken's new corporate work environment, where he interacted daily with strong businesswomen. He liked that he could talk to them, that they understood him, and that they had common interests. Not surprisingly, he found his female colleagues tempting. Some sensed his vulnerability and made strategic moves. Ken was forced to confront his situation and tell Sara how he felt. The gist of their talk was: I'm not happy. You're not happy. Why should we continue this? Sara didn't want a divorce, but Ken saw no other way. For a few months they tried to keep the marriage going until Ken succumbed to an overture from a woman at work. He knew it was a way to escape. Getting involved with another would be his ticket out the door. He was acknowledging that the marriage was over, and he hoped Sara would see it that way, too.

In Retrospect

If we reflect on the marriage of Ken and Sara, we see that a number of things went wrong that had nothing to do with either's worthiness. Ken had been immature the first time around, marrying a woman he hardly knew. Insecurity kept him from being independent and marrying from strength rather than weakness. He married to fill a hole in himself that arose from having been abandoned by a father who died, causing his family to disintegrate and him to splinter. Ken repeated the same orientation with Sara. Rather than spending time after his divorce to grow through the pain and disappointment and to allow himself to heal, he saw a chance to "fix" his messy life by marrying to blot out the reality of the first marriage and divorce. He chose a "plain Jane" woman who would not threaten to leave. Since "being left" was such a horrible part of his first marriage, Ken unknowingly sought a woman with one important trait—a dependent personality. He loved that she thought he was wonderful and that he wouldn't have to worry about her ever leaving him.

For her part, Sara liked being swept away from her smothering father. Ironically, the very things that attracted Ken to Sara—her youth and naiveté—and the things that attracted Sara to Ken—his take-charge personality—proved to be the undoing of their marriage. When confronted with the reality of their choices, both parties realized their mistakes.

Could their situation have been salvaged with marriage counseling? Maybe, but the important thing to recognize is that the marriage failed because each person married for the wrong reasons. For Ken, the failure to resolve the issues in his divorce drove him to remarry for the wrong reasons. For Sara, the search for a rescuer from a bad dad was a spurious reason at best.

In the story of Ken and Sara, the real reason for the divorce can be seen early on. As an independent observer, can you really conclude that this divorce occurred because Ken had a domineering manner, Sara was immature and naïve, the couple fought, or that Ken eventually had an affair? Or would you be more correct to say the divorce occurred because Ken and Sara were not ready to marry anyone? The fact is, when they did marry during a time when their circumstances prevented them from thinking clearly and making better choices, they both chose partners who were wrong for them. Today, both Ken and Sara are happily remarried. They are the same people with the same personalities and traits, but they found other spouses who reacted positively rather than negatively to their real selves.

Basically, the plot line of every rescue has someone looking for a savior to help make problems go away and a rescuer who wants to save someone for his or her own personal reasons. Such stories are common because recently divorced people are almost always in a needy, problem-plagued state, which makes them fair game for being salvaged by someone who enjoys projects.

Now, you may be saying, what's wrong with nurturing a partner in crisis? Absolutely nothing. In every healthy marriage, one partner will *want* and expect the other to take care of him (or her) when he faces a tough problem. So what's the difference? In an unhealthy marriage of rescue, one of the parties *needs* to have someone take care of her and the other *needs* to do it. One party is a leaner, and the other always gets leaned on. There is no quid pro quo. The basis for the marriage is this one mutual need.

I Can Fix That

The eldest of six children, Adriana grew up helping take care of her younger siblings. At age 35, she married Roger, a contractor and recovering alcoholic. As Roger's business became more successful, he became more of a workaholic. He and Adriana drifted apart. He didn't seem to need her anymore. They separated without much fanfare. After a 27-year marriage, they divorced. At first Adriana hardly noticed any difference in her life because she'd spent little time with Roger in recent years. But gradually reality hit, and she became despondent. Not even her enviable financial situation—a divorce settlement of more than three million dollars—provided much comfort.

Aware that she was a rather plain woman, Adriana suspected that the odds of her finding another husband at her age were not good. Soon, loneliness became one of her biggest enemies. Then Adriana's stockbroker introduced her to another client of his named Daniel, who was 64. He had been through some rough sledding in his business, and he was struggling emotionally and financially. The stockbroker gave Adriana a rundown of the situation, but he also thought they might be a companionable pair who could comfort each other. Much later Adriana found out that Daniel had been much worse off than the stockbroker had told her. Daniel had lost most of his assets, was deeply in debt, and his second wife had just left him. He also had a history of gambling problems. Daniel had tried counseling, but his addiction resurfaced whenever he got depressed. When Daniel met Adriana, he saw a quick fix.

Adriana knew about Daniel's problems because he talked about them constantly, which would have made most women run for cover. But not Adriana. Nothing turned her on like a good fixer-upper, and Daniel was indeed a challenge. When they went anywhere, she picked up the tab. She bought him clothes and gifts. She admitted to friends that because of her age, she surely had few options and thank goodness Daniel needed her. Within a year, the couple married. Adriana paid off Daniel's bills, bought him a new car, and moved him into her spacious home. Everything went well for a few years. Daniel appreciated Adriana's generosity, and the couple appeared to be very much in love. Then Daniel had a setback. He was diagnosed with prostate cancer. This condition brought back both his depression and his gambling addiction. Tension in the marriage grew, and within six months Adriana filed for divorce. Adriana was disappointed that her efforts to help Daniel hadn't worked, and she didn't want to be around to watch him go downhill into deeper depression and gambling, not to mention that it was also hard on her bank account. Still, though, she felt guilty about leaving Daniel, and she hated that she had failed in her efforts to help him overcome his problems.

What went wrong in this marriage? The story of Adriana and Daniel is as complicated as the situations in most remarriages and redivorces. Adriana had assumed she would have no problems because she figured her emotional state would be the same once she and Roger were divorced. Instead, she was lonely, which drove her to find a spouse replacement. Given her nature as a fixer of others' problems, she was vulnerable to someone like Daniel. Also, Adriana's belief that there were no men who would be interested in her at her age made her settle. She didn't believe she could be more selective.

So what can you learn from this story? Put this sticky note where you can see it daily: *When you make bad choices, you can expect bad outcomes.*

A Rescue by Any Other Name Is Still a Band-Aid

Why do some people rescue others? Don't be fooled into thinking rescuers are altruistic. If you're a rescuer, you may be so insecure that you search for someone to help or to fix because you're most comfortable with a relationship based on the premise of need. You look at the relationship in this way: If your partner needs you, he will appreciate you and be dependent on you. You will have some power and control over him, and you will feel content, knowing that your mate will not leave you.

Another reason for rescue is that you like the stimulation and the challenge. You aren't happy once a deal is done. The chase is fun and exciting, but once you reel in the prey, things grow mundane and boring.

Rescuers are rarely aware of their motivations. Most see themselves as do-gooders. It is true that some people have personalities oriented strongly toward helping other people, and there's nothing wrong with that. What is wrong is making your spouse selection based on a do-gooder project.

It's also important to know that when you locate a person who wants to be rescued, that individual is probably unstable. And we are not speaking exclusively of alcoholics, drug addicts, sexaholics, and other extreme cases. If the object of your affection has recently gone through a divorce, she is probably very needy due to loneliness, financial distress, or parenting strain. Your new love may be overwhelmed by problems and looking for a helpmate to fix the situation so she won't have to take on that overwhelming job herself. With this albatross around your partner's neck, she will be a taker in marriage—not a giver. The immense problems that are spin-offs of divorce may lead an otherwise self-sufficient person to become helpless and extremely vulnerable to a savior.

Are you interested in someone who is willing to settle for anyone who will problem-solve her out of her mess? Do you want to be chosen as a mate just for your helpfulness? And things can change. A friend of mine rescued a woman in distress who then got her act together and eliminated him from the picture. When she got her problems resolved, she told him, "I never loved you, and now I want a divorce."

Are You at Risk?

Are you at risk for rescuing someone or being rescued through marriage? Do you...

- have a history of rescuing people or being rescued by them?
- fear trusting again?
- feel more comfortable with someone who *needs* you to help him or has a dependent personality?
- never think you're actually self-sufficient?
- believe your problems are insurmountable, and you can't solve them on your own?
- have a dependent personality?

If you answered yes to a few of these, you may be at risk for the rescue scenario. *Instead of getting married to solve your problems,* here are some action steps to help you avoid this mistake.

For the Rescuer

Accept this truth: *You cannot fix another person.* This is a difficult lesson for people who are control freaks or caregivers who want everybody else to function properly. Only God can fix people.

Avoid what is bad for you. If you were addicted to an illegal substance, people would warn you to stay away from it. Likewise, if you know you have a history as a rescuer, you should stay away from people who need rescuing. One woman we counseled told us she knew that she was a "loser magnet." If that's you, remember that just because losers approach you doesn't mean you have to encourage them. You have the option of running the other way when they come around.

Understand the reasons you rescue. We are not head-shrinking here, but sometimes if you'll just be a bit introspective about your marital or family history, you can identify why you are attracted to people in distress. Write answers to these questions: Has someone abandoned you physically or emotionally? Have people you've "helped" in the past been more loyal to you? Make two headings: "a person who needs my help" and "a person who is self-sufficient." In each column write what you find appealing about each type of person as a spouse. Also, write what you find unappealing. Are you more comfortable with the needy person? If so, why? Once you have a better picture of your motivation, you may be less likely to repeat old patterns.

Concentrate on rebuilding your self-esteem. Your divorce and other people's reactions to it can make you feel like a loser. Drop friends and acquaintances who put you down. Make a list of all your great qualities and reread it often. Realize that sometimes divorces occur simply because you made a bad decision, not because you are a bad or flawed person.

Apply your rescue skills to people other than marriage prospects. If you enjoy helping people, do volunteer work for your church or a charitable organization. This is great therapy because it makes you focus on other people's problems instead of your own. In this setting, you can help people in need without the risk of marrying them!

Learn to trust. Divorce makes you fear trusting anyone again. Seeking a weak person to save via remarriage isn't a good substitute for learning to trust again. Instead, try to date someone long enough to get to know who that person is and something about his or her history. This will give you the confidence to know whether the person is trustworthy or not.

For the Rescuee

Accept this truth: *Another person can't fix you, and if you let someone try to do that, you will pay the price.* If you're in a crisis, remarrying will only add to your problems. When you're traumatized, you're not equipped emotionally for launching a new relationship. Why trade a short-term fix for a long-term problem?

Avoid what is bad for you. Don't allow yourself to be taken in by mortal saviors bearing gifts. If you're vulnerable, don't date until you're more stable. If you attract rescuers, be on guard and make a point of choosing other types of people to date.

Get help. You won't be vulnerable to being rescued if you have solved your own problems and are not in a needy state. If obligations and responsibilities are truly overwhelming you, don't hesitate to seek help. Besides asking family and friends, you can turn to community groups and churches that offer assistance. Ask around or look online for counseling services—financial, psychological, and parenting. Find other divorced people who can act as a support group for you. Join a divorce recovery group or attend a workshop. Pray and ask God to direct your path to solutions.

"I married because I was in love, but didn't know my husband was a pathological liar, a narcissist who wasn't capable of loving anybody very much. I thought I was getting married for the right reasons, but now I realize I was lonely, scared, and wanting someone to take care of me." S.Y.

~ ❧ ~

"I had two children, and it was very rare to meet someone who would even consider dating someone who did have children. Therefore, a feeling of 'gratitude' was created and then milked from me. Even though I never actually admitted to feeling that way, he could tell and manipulated me like I should have been or was desperate, when the fact was, I think I was being realistic and accepted the fact that a single parent was not in demand. I used to think he was settling when the fact was, I settled." R.T.

~ ❧ ~

"In the first marriage, I married out of a sense of obligation. In the second marriage, my business had failed, and an Asian woman took me in, along with three of my five children. That didn't last, either." B.H.

~ ❧ ~

"My ex-husband's wife and daughter had recently died within the same week—his wife from an illness and the daughter on the way to the funeral. It was tragic. He was lonely and broken, and so was I, coming off a recent divorce from my second husband. Getting married just seemed like the right thing to do. He helped me financially, and I helped him to survive the hardest time of his life. It just didn't work out." L.J.

~ ❧ ~

"I married against my better intuition that this person needed me, and this was a wrong reason to marry someone I did not know very well. I couldn't seem to convince this person that we should wait and get to know each other better. I realize that this person needed to be loved since I learned later that he was an alcoholic, and someone with this problem does have a difficult time knowing self-love. I have a tendency to feel sorry for such people and wish I could help them, but no one can but God." Y.G.

~ ❧ ~

"My recent ex was around at the time my first marriage was dissolving, seeming to be a friend to both of us. He not only offered advice to save the marriage, he said all the things I had longed to hear…that I was beautiful and smart and worth the effort. He also had issues of his own to deal with, and we leaned on each other in mutual need and support. Upon my separation, I moved back into my family home, where I suffered the same emotional abuse as I had growing up. Though I had a job, I didn't have enough money to get my own place, and he suggested that I move in with him. Our bond grew stronger despite some very serious problems. He was my only true ally, and I was his. We married a year after I moved in. I felt we were spiritually, not just physically, connected, and that our love would make everything all right. I couldn't have been more wrong, though I kept hoping. I felt both trapped and safe at the same time." N.K.

~ ❧ ~

"My ex was very needy. I felt he was overpowering but was flattered by his attention, gifts, and what seemed to be a real need to have me in his life. I was independent, on a career path, and confident in my future. I was not looking for a relationship, though the most important relationship in my life had just ended rather abruptly. I didn't think I was on the rebound, but here was a man who was really very kind and loving and would not take no for an answer. We were married within six months of first meeting." S.H.

～ ❧ ～

"After the breakup of my second marriage, I suffered a nervous breakdown. I was not able to work at the time because I was a truck driver and couldn't find adequate babysitting for my children. My three children then ranged in ages from three to fourteen. When my third wife and I met, she wasn't honest about her character, and I suppose I was an easy mark for her. After a year of living together, I thought I knew her well enough to marry, so we did. Looking back, I see that my mind wasn't clear enough to recognize the signs in her behavior that she wasn't honest with me or my children." B.J.

～ ❧ ～

"Seven years after my first divorce, my sons were teenagers. Having always found my identity by reverting to 'codependent care-taking,' I believe I married my second husband to fill a void caused when my sons needed me less. I really have no idea why he wanted to marry. He did like to be taken care of. Both husbands needed as much attention as a two-year-old. Although on the surface my second husband seemed worlds apart from the first, the very same unhealthy relationship patterns took place in both marriages. In my opinion, with both marriages, we unconsciously sought out people who would fill our needs, albeit unhealthy ones." L.L.

～ ❧ ～

"My ex-wife was blind and 100 percent dependent on me for assistance. I fulfilled a need that she had, and also one that I had of being the 'rescuer.' " V.P.

6
Wrong Reason #2
I'll Show You

❧ ❧ ❧

When a woman steals your husband,
there is no better revenge than
to let her keep him.

Let's make a list of all the problems people face when they get divorced. Well, okay, that list would take another book. But low self-esteem would be at the top of many people's list. It's a natural because, in divorce, someone usually rejects and the other person feels rejected. Guess which one has low self-esteem? When Ed's first wife left him and he got his divorce, he just knew he had a big "L" on his forehead screaming "loser, loser, loser." Some of the most self-confident people on the planet turn into mush when rejected by their spouses. We have seen extremely successful people reduced to whimpering shells of themselves. It really hurts when someone says she's leaving you. It hurts even more when she leaves you for someone else. If the person she leaves you for is more handsome or beautiful, it hurts. If the person is smarter or richer, it hurts. If the person is ugly, dumb, and poor, it hurts even more!

So what do you do about this kind of rejection? How do you respond to your ex and to others? That's the issue at the base of this wrong reason to remarry. Some people can't take rejection lying down. They want revenge. And this is a problem because if you marry another spouse to prove something to your ex or yourself, you're playing a dangerous game that will bite you. "I'll show my ex!" Sure, that runs through your mind, but what really happens is that your vindictive motives get in the way of the decisions you make. And you don't know what's best for you because you're not thinking straight. How can you be when your mind is churning with the idea of proving something?

Post-divorce revenge is waged far too often, and the results are often devastating. Just think of all the country-western songs that romanticize how a victim of cheating gets even with the cheater. It sounds good, and it makes you believe there could be poetic justice. But extracting a pound of flesh from your ex by doing something to show him that he was wrong is totally pointless. The revenge premise makes this much sense: "Watch me shoot myself in the foot. Then you'll see how desirable I am, and you'll wish you hadn't left me."

What should you do when you're rejected? Nothing. That's right—nothing. In fact, to heal fully from a divorce, you need to forgive your ex eventually. "Forgive?" you say. "Forget that!" But the simple truth is that anger, bitterness, and resentment can eat you up from the inside. Your ex doesn't suffer from your hostility, you do. So you must find a way to forgive your ex-spouse so that he or she no longer has a continuing hold on you. That enables you to get well. Forgiving is a decision, just like not forgiving is a decision (more on this later). The Bible says, "Go ahead and be angry. You do well to be angry—but don't use your anger as fuel for revenge. And don't stay angry. Don't go to bed angry. Don't give the Devil that kind of foothold in your life" (Ephesians 4:26-27 MSG).

The worst move of all is taking action to prove that your mate was wrong to abandon you and that you are indeed desirable. Maybe your fantasy is that you will show your ex that you can definitely get someone better-looking, smarter, richer. Marlene, whose story is recapped here, decided she wanted to prove something to her ex and to herself. Her motive to do this was so strong that she was willing to marry for the wrong reason just to drive home how right she was.

Marlene's Revenge

"That *snake!* Sterling left me for that skinny secretary of his, and now I'm going to show him." So were the fatal words of sweet Marlene. Well, she wasn't really even all that sweet. In fact, Marlene had a wicked temper, and she didn't like to get bested by anyone.

Marlene and Sterling had met and married while attending college. They were both art majors, and they opened a gallery after graduation. Their natural tendency to be competitive served them well in building the business; unfortunately, they became so competitive with each other that Marlene had to stop working at the gallery.

When Sterling left her after admitting his affair, Marlene was mortified. What would her friends think? They would think she was a nagging wife. They would think she was over the hill. Marlene admitted that she didn't really care that Sterling was gone because their marriage hadn't been going well for years. They led separate lives. The problem for her was how he left. Why didn't he just ask for a divorce? Marlene's vengeful lament: "By going off with that bimbo, he made a fool of me. I can't just let this stand. The whole world knows what happened."

During the months Marlene waited for the divorce to be final, she began a makeover crusade. She had cosmetic surgery, an image update, new hair color and styling—the works. When finished, she focused on changing her environment. She redecorated the house, bought a fancy car, and purchased a new wardrobe. She was ready to rumble.

The war began. Marlene called everyone she knew asking for names of men she could approach. She even used her creative talents to begin bizarre activities to entrap a man. Marlene would watch the obituaries and send a cake to any man who had lost his wife if he sounded prosperous. All this activity began to pay off. Marlene's social life became a whirlwind of dating and partying. She blatantly talked about her conquests, single and married. Soon Sterling heard about her exploits and called Marlene to tell her she was making a fool of herself. A few of the older men she dated expressed serious interest in her, but she waved off any chance of marriage.

But then a friend introduced her to Ron, a very handsome younger man who had everything going for him except brains. He had always gotten by on his looks. After a few dates with Marlene, he saw his future in her checkbook and pursued her with a vengeance. He flattered her constantly and insisted on escorting her to functions where they would be seen in public. Marlene's friends, with raised eyebrows, took her aside and asked her what she was thinking. Her best friend even told her Ron was just after her money. Marlene would hear none of it. Getting married to Ron was just the vindication she needed. She proposed to him, and they got married a few months later. At first, everything seemed to go well, surprising everyone. But that didn't last. The marriage ended ten months later when Marlene filed for divorce. Ron claimed the problem was Marlene's temper. She was demanding, and when she didn't get her way, she unloaded with a screaming fit. She said the marriage ended because she couldn't take Ron's endless spending. She said, "I didn't want a gigolo; I wanted a husband."

Costly Eye Candy

Marlene's need to prove something to her ex put her in jeopardy from the start. She was vulnerable to anyone who made her look desirable. That Ron was "eye candy" made him the perfect marriage prospect because that's what she needed to prove something to herself and to her ex. Even knowing that he was a gold-digger didn't stop this marriage from happening. Marlene knew better, but she went ahead because having a successful marriage wasn't her main objective. She wanted a new husband who would help her make a point. Once that point was made, she didn't need the marriage to continue. So when the inevitable problems occurred, she bailed.

It goes without saying that Ron got what he asked for, too—a woman with money. The very thing he found appealing about Marlene—her money—proved to be what later divided them. Ron and Marlene's story marriage was doomed—DOA—when they exchanged vows. When you remarry for the wrong reason, you are likely to end up redivorced and go through the heartache, embarrassment, and healing all over again.

You're the Victim of Your Revenge

When people hurt, a natural reaction is to strike out. Do not get married to get revenge against your ex; to prove to yourself, your ex, and your friends that you are desirable; or to win the "game" by showing your ex you can snag someone even more desirable than him or her. These are definitely the drivers behind many remarriages. When your emotions are damaged by rejection, you may focus on revenge, and you're drawn toward irrational behavior.

What should you do when you have been rejected? The answer again: Do nothing to prove anything. Ask God to help you see your ex as He sees him. One reason some people seek revenge is that, in addition to feeling rejected and insecure, they assume they are to blame. They need to "fix" the problem and find someone to validate them.

You may be placing blame on yourself for marriage failure if your self-talk sounds like any of the following:

> He or she would have stayed with me...
> > if I were more beautiful.
> > if I were more intelligent.
> > if I were more loving.
> > if I had been a better lover.
> > if I had been less demanding.
> > if I had been a better cook.
> > if I had been a better provider.
> > if I had been more helpful around the house.

And your conjecture and self-flagellation can go on and on forevermore.

In our divorce recovery groups, we hear these things over and over. When a spouse leaves us, we look for reasons, and we blame ourselves. What about your ex? Could she have a problem? He abandoned you. She didn't try to work it out. He had a midlife crisis. She had an affair. Or maybe you can't even pinpoint why your ex rejected you and dissolved the marriage. The main point is: When you feel rejected, you need to give yourself time to heal. Lean on the support of friends who will reassure you of your value and desirability. And never consider marriage when you're in this low and unpredictable state of mind. Remember: *If you feel less than, you will be willing to settle for someone less than.*

Some people ask, "How do you know when the motives for marriage are wrong?" That's a tough question because we all want certain benefits to come from getting married, and the benefits we seek are sometimes self-serving. You're looking for a person who will take care of you in a loving way, right? But you can tell if your motives for marriage are wrong by having a clear enough mind to know the difference. To have a clear mind, you must make sure you have healed sufficiently from your divorce so that you don't *need* to get remarried, but instead *want* to remarry. That can only happen with time. Marlene didn't allow herself the time nor did she spend the energy to grieve, to forgive, and to heal. Because this process wasn't completed, she couldn't approach a new relationship from a healthy perspective. If you don't allow yourself time to grieve, forgive, and heal, you may well find yourself behaving in ways that are not in your own best interest just like Marlene did. You deserve better, and that can only happen when you recognize that revenge and vindication will make matters worse for you.

Are You at Risk?

If you can relate to the story of Ron and Marlene, or you're concerned that you might marry on the rebound to prove something, ask yourself these questions, all of which show the potential for hasty, revenge-led remarriage. Do you...

- feel crushed by rejection, have shattered self-esteem, believe that no one would want you?
- need to get even with your ex for the injustice and hurt perpetrated?
- know you can't rest until you prove you were right and your ex was wrong?
- play competitive games in your mind with your ex?
- want to prove to yourself that you have value to someone?
- want to get remarried because your ex did?

Some people solve these needs by marathon dating or, worse, by sleeping around. This just postpones or sidesteps the necessary healing process. Don't fall into the trap of trying to one-up your ex by proving he or she was stupid to leave you. The root causes of behaving this way are the insecurities that rejection engenders. How can you overcome these feelings without marathon dating, aggressive pursuit of sex, and other self-destructive behaviors? How can you resolve this situation without remarrying on the rebound?

Get perspective on any affair, marriage, and divorce. About 70 percent of divorces involve a third party. Accept that an affair is a cruel way to end a marriage, but also that it may not be the real cause of the marriage's failure. Refocus by listing things that went wrong during the marriage. Acknowledge your part as well as your partner's. This helps you see the broader picture rather than simply focusing on the ugly stuff that often accompanies the end of a marriage.

Take a timeout. By recognizing that your immediate response to the situation is to get even or prove something, allow a cooling-off period for yourself, during which time you will do nothing: no dating, no unkind behavior, no vindictive actions. During this time pamper yourself. Be a little self-centered.

Stop asking about your ex. Do you want to know everything your ex is doing? Do you ask friends to tell you who your ex is dating? Do you grill your children for tidbits about your ex? You have to stop. This can make you crazy and lead you to "compete" and attempt to prove something. Tell anyone who offers "ex sightings" or similar information that you don't want to hear it. Discourage gossipers from using you as a sounding board about your ex. The less you know, the better.

Spend time with supportive friends and family. Avoid negative people. Iron sharpens iron according to Scripture. You need to rebuild your self-confidence, and one healthy way to do that is to allow your good friends and family to reassure you that you are indeed okay. If you have friends of the opposite sex who won't misunderstand your motives, spend some time with them, too. Avoid those people who want to blame you for your divorce or your present situation.

When Ed got divorced, he discovered that some "friends" had their own agendas. "One couple was angry that they would no longer have my wife and me to socialize with, so they went on a tirade about what I did to cause my divorce. Another couple had their own marital problems, and my split threatened their situation so they lashed out at me."

Find healthy ways to reduce your anger. Unresolved anger is one significant cause of trying to get even or prove something to an ex. Do physical workouts or deep-breathing exercises. Listen to soft music, read humorous books, and get sufficient rest. Remove belongings of your ex that will rekindle your anger. Try new things and go new places. Get counseling for anger management if you can't overcome hostile feelings on your own.

Shift your thinking to the future. If you concentrate on the past, what can change? Make an effort to stop talking and thinking about your divorce and your ex. Grieving is good; dwelling is bad. Set new goals for yourself. The simple act of setting goals forces you to think about the future rather than be stuck in the past.

"I had just moved back to my hometown and had been divorced for five years. I wanted a stable home for my three teens and me. I was not in love and was tired of struggling alone. I met a man in September, and we got married in July. I really did not know him at all. I wanted to prove to all my friends and family that I could find a husband. But it only led to problems and divorce." T.D.

"I believe that I had something to prove to myself. My previous spouse was of a different race, and I was trying to 'get back in' with my race. This was another reason why I married for a third time. Also, my last spouse was dating a person of another race who was married, and deep inside I resented this fact." L.W.

"Neither of our first marriages worked out. A month after our divorce, my husband remarried. I married on the rebound after I heard he got married. We just never should have married. None of my family liked him, and after we married, he started seeing other women but told me I didn't know what I was talking about. There is no romance or loving between us. He claimed he loves me, but he never shows that he loves me. Now we are staying together because I can't afford to live on my own so it's better to stay together money-wise." M.H.

"I was married for ten years. At the beginning it was a true love story that ended soon when we got kids. And with them financial problems came. Then we divorced in haste, not thinking much about the children. My ex said that I would crawl back to him and beg him to return, but I didn't! I rushed to the altar a second time only to be divorced in two years. I have been divorced for twenty years and haven't tried to get married again." S.F.

~ ❧ ~

"I married because I was in love with him. He, apparently, married me to prove to himself, family, and friends that he could catch a winner. Everyone had told him for the seven years that we dated that I was too good for him…and he could never end up with a girl like me. We married (second marriages for both of us) in a big church wedding, in front of all our family and friends. Then, after one month of wedded bliss, I found out that he was romancing another woman…in my new home! I guess his game was cat and mouse. As long as he was pursuing, he was very attentive and interested. Once I said 'I do,' the game was over, and he was on to bigger and better things! I hung in trying to do my part and make it work but to no avail. I divorced him after fourteen months of marriage." V.L.

~ ❧ ~

"Marriage number one, I was sixteen and pregnant. Number two, my ex convinced me that no one would ever want me or the kids. I got married to prove him wrong. Marriages three and four, I was very lonely. I have been divorced and have not remarried." B.G.

~ ❧ ~

"I had a small child. My next husband was a very good-looking man, and I had friends who said he would never marry me. I guess to begin with I kind of set out to prove them wrong. I then decided that I wanted to further my education. He felt no need for that. I was to stay the ol' barefoot and pregnant wife. And I saw no need for that. I found myself in a rut. Get up, fix breakfast, send hubby off to work, feed children, send one off to school, entertain one toddler, clean house, wash clothes, pay bills, diaper infant, cook dinner. I could go on forever. I finally packed up and left. I went to school and raised my children." J.S.

7
Wrong Reason #3
Stop the Dating Game

❧ ❧ ❧

I've been on so many blind dates
I should get a free dog.

WENDY LEIBMAN

Dating. That's one of the scariest things that divorced or widowed people face.

Divorcing or losing a spouse after 18 years of marriage, you know that you're definitely no kid, but now you're being tossed back into the world of dating and courtship and relationship games. You have obligations and commitments. You're a respected citizen of the community. The only intimacy you've known for the past 18 years was with your spouse. And now you are supposed to revert to the way you were as a teenager who went on dates.

Seventeen Again

This is almost too frightening to contemplate. Even if you are newly divorced or just in the process, a maddening thought lurks in the back of your brain: I'll have to kiss a stranger! And since we aren't kids, this "date" may expect me to have a physical relationship. You may be thinking that you simply can't handle the thought of dating. You truly believed that you would never have to go through that painful process again. Also, you hate the idea of having to try so hard. You don't look like you did before…a little heavier, balder, etc. Now you have to make yourself look desirable again. You have to compete. Then there's also the issue of finding someone to date. How do you meet people? Singles groups, church socials, clubs, the Internet? Just hide out at home and hope someone comes by? The options are not good when you're used to having a mate who is always there. Friends might fix you up, but most of the people you know are married, so they don't have a long list of singles in their social circles.

In reality, you're going to be in the good company of lots of people who are single, divorced, and widowed in the United States, which is almost half of the adult population. People in divorce recovery groups get a shock when they come and see so many people going through the trial of divorce just like they are. If you're newly divorced and don't think you're ready to date, then don't do it yet! However, if you have been divorced for five years or more and haven't dated because you are afraid, drum up some courage and get out there. About 80 percent of divorced people remarry (the percentage is higher if you're young), so you are very likely to marry again if you are open to it. Dating can actually be a pleasant experience. The divorced people who are like you won't judge you because they understand what it's like to be divorced and dating again. You get to meet new people who will be interested in learning about you.

The Dating Disease

The problem with dating is that people often get impatient. They get what we call the "dating disease." There are three versions of this illness:

1. *One-stop dating.* Since you hate the thought of dating, you grab the first person who comes along. Or maybe you just wait to be chosen by someone. When he or she asks, you say yes.

2. *Mission dating.* You hate being single so you are on a mission to marry. You talk about marriage on the first date. Only desperate dates are not frightened off by this behavior.

3. *Marathon dating.* You're looking for Mr. or Ms. Perfect (the opposite of the way your ex was). You date frantically—as many as you can pack into a week. You date so much for so many years that you finally tire of the game. When you burn out, you settle for someone who isn't the best for you.

Remarriage—the Easy Way

Deana was a sophisticated woman who lived in a beautiful neighborhood in an upscale part of town. Her husband was a successful entrepreneur who had started a chain of carpet stores. She had an extensive social life in the upper echelons of society. Deana had what she thought was a happy marriage of 37 years until one day when her husband came home and informed her that he'd been having a relationship with a man he'd met in his business. Deana was devastated. She felt sure that this hurt more and was more embarrassing than if he'd had an affair with a woman.

When I met Deana in a divorce recovery group, her divorce had been final for more than two years, but she was still in tears. She said that she never used the word "divorced" with friends or acquaintances. She just couldn't bring herself to vocalize the reality of her status. In her mind, she was not divorced or single; she was just in transition—between marriages. No amount of reality therapy could make her look realistically at her situation. The thought of dating was abhorrent. Deana refused to subject herself to "that kind of adolescent abuse." She faced quite a dilemma. Here was a woman who wanted a spouse replacement but wasn't willing to date.

Not long after, a female acquaintance of Deana passed away suddenly and unexpectedly. Deana called the husband to offer condolences. Tom had been married 40 years, and he was lost without his wife. Tom and Deana began talking frequently by phone. She helped him find various services he needed. She helped him clean out his deceased wife's belongings. Soon they began having dinner together. Within two months, they announced their engagement. They told their friends how lucky they were to find each other. Both seemed pleased that serendipity had allowed them to avoid the unpleasant necessity of dating a variety of strangers. They had remarried the easy way.

Less than two years after the marriage was consummated, Deana filed for divorce. She never said why the marriage failed, but few of her friends were surprised. The problem boiled down to insufficient healing. She was not ready to remarry, but she did anyway. While Deana had been divorced for two years, she had not been willing to face the reality of being divorced and single again. Thus she found it impossible to go through the steps required to heal and move forward. When you live in the past, it is impossible to grow in the present or future. Obviously she dragged the pain of her prior divorce into the new marriage. Two years seems like a long time, but it takes some people longer than others to come to terms with their circumstances.

Tom's situation was just as bad. After 40 years of marriage, two months wasn't nearly long enough to grieve the loss of his wife. These two merged as basket cases, which was not conducive to starting a healthy new marriage. When you've known someone as a single or single-again for only a few months, you cannot know that person well enough to determine whether he or she is suitable for you as a marriage partner. Yet many men marry within a year of divorce. Big, unpleasant surprises are likely to be your fate when you marry that quickly.

Marathon Dating Burnout

Gerald had been divorced four times when we met him. He had just married Meredith. We asked him how they met, why he chose her, and how it all had happened. He told us that they had signed up for a dating service. Gerald was in his fifties; Meredith was in her late forties. She'd had a long first marriage and a nasty, prolonged divorce.

Both Gerald and Meredith were successful businesspeople who loved to socialize. He had been single for six years and she for five.

They had both dated many people during this period. Through friends, relatives, parties, business acquaintances, and dating services, they had made the rounds. But Gerald confided that he had grown tired of running around. "What might seem exciting to some of my married friends who envied my single lifestyle got old quickly," he said. When Gerald and Meredith met through the dating service, they had an instant subject in common. Most people they had dated were not as successful as they were. In fact, they had concluded that the world of divorced people was made up of a lot of losers. The other thing they had in common was that they were very tired of the dating game. They discussed this for hours—how frustrated they were and how painful it was to date losers and waste their time night after night. They decided to end the dating whirlwind and get married. Why not? They seemed compatible. They had a mutual respect for each other's accomplishments and money-making abilities. And they were tired of searching. It seemed rational.

The marriage did last four years. However, their respective jobs kept them so occupied that they never actually moved in together. They kept their separate homes. Had they moved into one home, the marriage probably would have lasted four weeks. What went wrong? They had married because marathon dating led to burnout. Marathon dating usually signals that a person is extremely unhappy with his current situation, and that's not a great position for making a marriage decision. You may believe that you can fill the hole in your life by dedicating your energy toward the search for a replacement spouse. Gerald and Meredith urgently wanted to avoid being alone and wanted to get married. Some people agree to marry the first person who asks. What prevented this from happening with Gerald and Meredith was that each had a feeling of superiority that made it impossible to be open to anyone not of the same economic level.

In truth, many divorced people carry around tons of baggage and are so unhealed that the term "walking wounded" fits perfectly. Some are looking for saviors to pull them out of their despair and hardships. You would be wise to avoid such people. At the same time, don't make the mistake of thinking that just because a prospective spouse has the same income-earning ability you do, that's a great basis for marriage. Because Gerald and Meredith were utterly disappointed that they had failed to find winner mates in the sea of dating, they were primed for ending the race. Each wanted to get off the merry-go-round and grabbed the first person who looked promising. What they had in common was frustration, and that's not a good basis for a happy marriage. When this couple decided to get married with little real knowledge about each other, only dumb luck or very hard work would have made that relationship match work.

Takeaway Knowledge

Dating as an adult can be hard, and dating as a senior adult can be even harder because it has been so many years since you've been single. When something you do causes pain or discomfort, you naturally want to avoid it or get it over with as quickly as possible. Herein lies the risk of dating after divorce. Some people are vulnerable to marriage proposals just because they love the idea of never having to date again. Others overactively date and get married just to end the dating game. When either one of these flawed reasons leads to remarriage, intuition, common sense, and perceptiveness are out the window.

When dating is a game, there is an inherent problem. In contrast, if you're picky about the people you choose to date, you won't be driven to date as many people as possible. If you date just to have an enjoyable evening, you'll have pleasant experiences that won't seem like chores. You will not have unrealistic expectations that lead to unending disappointments. Nor will you become jaded and worn out. On the other hand, if you make dating a mad marathon—a game to be won or lost by quickly finding Mr. or Ms. Right—you set yourself up for frustration and the increased chance that you will grab someone (sometimes anyone) just to end the pain.

Are You at Risk?

If you feel you have any form of dating disease, you are not ready to remarry. Do you...

• have a major fear of dating?

- date like you're on a mission to marry?
- marathon-date, seeing as many people as possible?
- experience extreme frustration that you have not found a new spouse?

Here are some steps you can take to cure the dating disease.

Take a break. When you're in a frenzy, you have no clear perspective on what you're doing.

If you are marathon dating, decide to refrain from going out on dates for at least three months.

Analyze why you're on a mission. During your time-out, figure out why your frustration level is driving you so hard toward a pay-dirt marriage moment. Get input from close friends who will be honest with you. Why have you dated so many people without connecting with someone? Are you dating the wrong people? Are you sending the wrong signal, such as desperation? Are you afraid to allow someone to get close again? Are you terribly lonely? Do you just hate being single?

Be more selective. Make a list of the things that are important to you in a spouse. Before dating someone, find out whether the person is a viable prospect by reviewing your criteria. Refuse to date anyone who falls seriously short. Ask friends to fix you up with quality dates.

Develop a broader social circle. Often extensive dating is a cover-up for a lack of a social life. If you have few friends to be with, you may try to overcome loneliness with a raft of dates.

Climb the ladder. If you are afraid of heights, you have to climb a ladder to prove to yourself you can do it. If you're afraid to date, face your fears and take the first step. Don't back off just because you've had a few unpleasant dating experiences. Every outing may not produce the love of your life, but you may have some interesting conversation or find a new circle of friends. Find a reputable dating service and take a chance.

"I was tired of being single and dating for so many years and wanted to believe that this fellow was truthful about his indiscretions and wanted to start anew. This was not the case. He simply wanted a maid to wait on his every whim and be totally in control of everything. He then proceeded to start an online affair with a gal and went there to carry out the affair. We divorced, and I left that state. I don't know to this day whatever happened to the relationship." P.K.

"I was sick of the bars and everyone hitting on me at work. He felt the same way. We had both been married before and had both been divorced about the same number of years. I was divorced for fourteen years from my first marriage, and he had been divorced twelve years. We seemed to have a lot in common, and we both were ready to settle down and try again." L.S.

"I had broken up with my boyfriend....I was tired of the bar scene, tired of the dating scene. My kids were gone from home. A man talked me into going to Kansas for a new start. He promised me the moon, but I didn't know I had to pay for it. After being in Kansas about four months, I knew I'd made a mistake in marriage and the move. But I didn't want to go back to single life, so I stayed with him for seven years." R.G.

"I was quite lonely and tired of dating. I was in the military. I thought I knew her quite well, but things changed after she got pregnant. We worked through it. But it didn't matter what I did—I was always in the wrong. We kept it going because of the kids for as long as I could." W.M.

8
Wrong Reason #4
Somebody's Going
to Move in Here

❧ ❧ ❧

*Getting married for sex
is like buying a 747 for the free peanuts.*

JEFF FOXWORTHY

A divorced acquaintance, Brian, bought a new house. Before he moved in, he casually mentioned, "Somebody's going to move in here with me. I'm not going to move into this big house by myself." What was so surprising about this statement was that he wasn't even dating anyone special at the time. But loneliness after divorce can be a killer. When you have been married for a number of years, it can be a great shock to find yourself alone, despite the fact that marriages in their last days are often quite lonely. The amazing part is the lengths that some people will go to, even to the extent of sticking their heads in the sand and ignoring all good advice and logic, just to "implant" a mate in that vacancy once again.

Brian Loved Being Married

Brian loved being married—again and again. Brian came from a poor family, and he had an unhappy childhood. His parents often fought about their lack of money. Children made fun of Brian because he never had the clothes, toys, and other things kids his age had. As an adult, the memory of that rejection drove him to find a way to gain recognition and respect from others. He did this by making money (earning and spending it) his primary focus. This display of riches proved quite an attraction to certain women. Not being an unusually handsome man, Brian still had little trouble getting women to show marriage interest.

In his first and second marriages, money issues were a problem, which caused him to stay single for a few years. But gradually Brian became more and more unhappy with his circumstances. He dated a few women whom friends had recommended, but none of the relationships went anywhere. Finally, his cousin told him about a beautiful single woman who worked at his company. Brian and this woman hit it off right from the start. In a few months they were engaged and planning to marry the next year. In anticipation of the marriage, Brian sold his home and purchased a larger place for them to live because he didn't want his new wife to feel as if she were moving into his place. A new house would be "their" home.

Then disappointment struck. Fifteen days before the wedding, the bride-to-be told Brian she changed her mind. They had purchased rings, and the wedding invitations had been sent. This was a devastating event because Brian had been very excited about the upcoming marriage. Plus, it was a massive blow to his ego to be rejected so publicly. Brian went into a tailspin. But he still planned to move into the new home because his old house was sold. That's when he said he would not move in alone. He would find someone to move in with him, and he had just two weeks to do it.

So Brian went to a singles bar where he met Sherry, who was young, attractive, and promiscuous. She looked good on a man's arm but admitted she never stayed there very long. Ignoring the fact that she didn't even try to hide who she was, he decided to marry her and make her the one to fill the spot in the new house. Many of Brian's friends tried to talk him out of this misadventure, but he was determined. He did not plan to be alone in that behemoth house. For her part, Sherry was willing to move in with no strings attached, but Brian wanted to get married so things would "look right" to his family. Although his children were grown, they would have been upset to hear that their father was playing house.

It didn't take long for the marriage to unravel. Sherry grew restless, and to get out of the house, she went back to her former career as a nurse. She began to arrive home later and later. Finally, it all blew up when Brian gave her an ultimatum, and she responded by leaving for good.

Brian succumbed to the pressure of loneliness. If you ask Sherry why the marriage ended, she would tell you Brian was suffocating her. Brian, on the other hand, would say that Sherry wasn't able to commit. Both of these statements are true. But that's not why the marriage failed. It was DOA when Brian asked Sherry to marry him. Brian knew what she was like from the start, but he paid no attention to signs that warned the marriage wouldn't work. Neither person was ready to marry anyone. In their condition, they were unable to be good marriage partners.

Going from Marriage Lonely to Single Lonely and Back Again

One of the loneliest feelings is being lonely in a bad marriage. As a marriage disintegrates, you usually have some emotional distance that goes on for weeks, months, or years. So when the marriage ends, you experience a sense of relief simply because you have felt alone for so long already. The only upside is that now you can enjoy the companionship of the opposite sex without cheating. That relief, though, can quickly end when you come home night after night to an empty house.

Mother Teresa was once asked what she thought was the greatest problem on the planet. No doubt the interviewer expected her to say disease, famine, or brutality. Instead she said loneliness. It was her belief that more people are in dark despair because they are removed from human contact and companionship. Many scientific experiments have shown that deprivation from human contact, emotional and physical, can drive a person mad. We are social creatures who need other people. Even introverts need contact with others.

Are You Happy or Are You Married?

The Three Stooges asked, "Are you happy or are you married?" You can be single and happy as easily as you can be married and unhappy. You've been married, and you know the benefits of a good marriage. But you're probably also familiar with the horrors of a bad one. Those downsides are important to remember because divorced people sometimes sentimentalize the institution of marriage and mistakenly decide that marriage is necessary for happiness. Bear in mind that if that were true, we wouldn't see so many people trying to get out of marriages. Meanwhile, the people who left marriages are now trying to get back in. Are we just insane creatures who forget the madness of a bad marriage and head right back for more of that special brand of misery? No, it's more like we remember only the good parts. After all, marriage, at its best, offers a tremendous support system to help us function effectively in daily life. Probably that's why married people live longer than divorced/single people. You enjoy having someone to share dreams and disappointments. You have a mate to love—and someone who loves you and cares for you.

Even as a divorced person you can take care of these emotional and physical needs. If you fail to do so, you may feel desperate for attention, which makes you vulnerable to marrying for the wrong reasons. We're not saying that marrying to gain human companionship is wrong—quite the contrary. The Bible says: "Therefore a man shall leave his father and mother and be joined to his wife, and they shall become one flesh" (Genesis 2:24 NKJV).

When you fail to solve your needs in a healthy way and you deprive yourself, you may try to get those needs met in ways that aren't in your best interest long-term. That's what loneliness can do. It can drive you to marry before you're ready. The key to avoiding this? Admit that you have needs and find ways to fill them without desperate measures.

Widow and Widower's Rebound

Divorce isn't the only thing that can give you foggy thinking. In the same way that divorced people have bouts of loneliness, so do widows and widowers, who have the same potential for making mistakes in choosing to marry for wrong reasons. Widowed people are left with many of the same emotional wounds as divorced people. Their situation differs mainly in that they don't have to cope with such strong feelings of guilt or rejection.

Jennifer, married for 26 years to an older man, had a perfectly wonderful marriage. When he died, she was grief-stricken—upset that her husband was gone, miserable that she was alone, and frustrated to be single again. For three years she avoided dating and kept herself busy.

Eventually Jennifer began to date, but her efforts were disappointing. Men had trouble with her stand on sex. As a Christian, her religious convictions made sex outside of marriage impossible for her. In a culture so sexually charged that many singles expect to go to bed together after dinner or a movie, she felt out of step. Meanwhile, Jennifer longed for the hugs, kisses, romance, and intimacy she had experienced with her husband. How could she make that happen again when even some Christian men she dated weren't willing to wait for the altar?

Just when things were beginning to look very dismal, Jennifer's pastor introduced her to a man who occasionally went to their church. Clay was a mature, recent widower. He had an excellent reputation and shared Jennifer's religious values. While they were dating, each believed that the other would make the perfect mate.

Though normally a clear-headed, logical person, Jennifer responded with teenager-like naiveté when Clay proposed to her. She agreed to marry him a few months later. She had noticed a very significant red flag, but it didn't fit her needs to address it. Clay's adult children, who had recently lost their mother, were totally opposed to the marriage. They waged an all-out effort to sabotage the wedding plans. They begged their father not to marry and told him that he would destroy the family if he brought in this outsider. They even threatened to have nothing to do with him if he went through with it.

This tirade bothered Jennifer, but she refused to be alone any longer and still believed Clay was the one. A few weeks after the wedding, Clay told Jennifer he had made a mistake. He missed his children and grandchildren and wanted the marriage annulled.

Jennifer had known up front that Clay's children were a major problem, but she wrongly assumed Clay could endure their rejection or that he and she would eventually win them over and the stresses would go away. Maybe if they had dated longer, the children would have changed their minds. Or, if they had dated longer, she would have gotten to know Clay better and learned his weaknesses and his low level of commitment to her. For Clay's side of it, he should have realized that his children had his best interests at heart and didn't want him to marry too quickly. Sometimes people who know you well can see what you fail to see because you're wearing emotional blinders. At any rate, ignoring his kids' protests proved unwise. Clay went through with the marriage, and then lived to regret it.

Did We Learn Anything?

Both marriages discussed in this chapter failed because the partners ignored the problems they saw brewing that could significantly damage the marriages. Why do people choose to overlook realities? Why do we minimize problems staring us right in the face? The reason is that it's often not expedient to face the truth. When we are plagued by loneliness, we will suspend good judgment and make decisions we would never consider otherwise.

What's the answer? Solve your loneliness problem in another way. Marriage isn't the only way to get companionship, hugs, and love. And having sex outside marriage isn't the answer, either. Many divorced people charge right out and jump into a sexual relationship as soon as the ink is dry on the divorce papers (some even before).

Others go from one sexual encounter to another. But if you've ever tried this, you know that serial sex is rarely satisfying. At first it's good for your post-divorce deflated ego; you like knowing that you've found someone who wants you. But whether you're male or female, you soon develop an empty feeling and maybe some pangs of guilt. You may even feel used. The main thing that you get from lots of sex without love or commitment is an underscoring of what's missing in your life—bona fide caring. The contrast of sex with and without love is startling, and that can increase your urge to marry even more. However, as we all know, getting married does not guarantee love, commitment, or a long-term relationship. That only happens when both you and your partner think you have found the right person and neither of you wants to be with anyone else. A marriage license only signifies a promise that two people make; it can't enforce it. If you are tempted to have unfettered sex with someone you're not married to, recognize the risks emotionally, spiritually, and physically. Our advice: Solve your loneliness problem another way.

Are You at Risk?

Here are some clues that you may be susceptible to marital blindness caused by loneliness. Do you…

- *frequently* have extreme feelings of loneliness (everyone does occasionally)?
- have friends tell you you're acting needy?
- think you can't be without someone in your life, whether he or she is coming or going?
- believe you can't live alone?
- find yourself on a constant mission to move in with someone?

If you see that you're developing "marital blindness" based on your answers to these questions, then you may want to work on strategies for avoiding singledom's loneliness. Find ways to have a life. Try these ideas.

Acknowledge that you are divorced and single. Amazingly, many divorced people refuse to take that step. How can you be happy and take full advantage of being single if you fight your status and continue to think of yourself as married—but missing a spouse?

Accept that some of your married friends may distance themselves from you. Married people sometimes act like they are threatened by newly single friends. Others feel awkward about your split, suspecting that they no longer have much in common with you. Accept that you will keep those friends who come through for you and be willing to let the rest go. Be realistic about the necessity of making an effort to find new, single friends. You have plenty of prospects out there. Thirty-five million divorced and widowed people live in the U.S., and many of those are looking for new friends, too.

Make the decision that you're going to understand what single life offers and capitalize on it. You cannot enjoy life when you are trying to be something you're not, looking over your shoulder, or wishing for something in the past. Tell yourself the truth: The past is in your past. Try to talk to as many people as you can find who are involved in the single community. Get involved.

Get a clear understanding of your need for other people. Some divorced people really are just fine being home with the kids or going to the movies by themselves, and that's great. But many others have much stronger "adult people" needs. If you fall into the latter category and you fail to get these needs met, you may end up in a dangerously needy situation. If you know that you need to be around people, make plans in advance for weekends, holidays, and other times when you don't want to be alone.

Today, women are just as likely as men to ask out the opposite sex. If you grew up in a more conservative time, you may be shocked at first if a woman asks you out. Rather than be repulsed, be flattered. Don't interpret it negatively, as if the woman were "coming on" to you. Girl-asks-boy is quite okay today. If you need to hug a member of the other gender, find appropriate friends who will respond to that need and not misinterpret it. If you need a sexual outlet, that issue is more difficult because casual sex isn't the answer. You can be sure that having a physical relationship with a friend irrevocably alters the dynamics between you, and usually you can't go back. This can be a quick way to lose a friend. Don't be tempted. Retain your values knowing God will honor them.

Go cold turkey. If you are a person who can't live alone, it's probably a good idea to force yourself to do it. Make a plan to live alone for at least a year. Get a dog or cat if you have no children at home. A pet gives you something to hug, and it will love you back.

Plan your evenings. Nighttime is often hard for a divorced person. You're probably busy during the day just like you always were, but at night, things are different. In our divorce recovery groups, we recommend that people develop an evening social life. Join groups that meet at night. Invite people over a few nights a week, especially on weekends and holidays.

Make a list of things you can do when you feel lonely. Keep this list handy and add to it over time so that you have it whenever you're bothered by feelings of loneliness. Develop some coping strategies. Go to the mall. You don't have to buy anything; just get out among people. Or call friends and talk just to have human contact. You will find various strategies like this can work when you are feeling disconnected from others and especially lonely.

Bottom line: If you are happy and content as a single person, you won't be tempted to marry the wrong person for the wrong reasons. This is just common sense. A happy single will only want to give up what he or she has if getting married offers something more. This keeps you thinking straight about marriage prospects and the inevitable pros and cons of such a decision. It also ensures that you're probably not going to ignore red flags just because of loneliness.

"We were two lonely people who married much too quickly and for all the wrong reasons—period." R.J.

~ ❧ ~

"I married because I didn't want to be alone, because I didn't want to take care of myself, because I was damaged and I thought another relationship could fix it. Boy, was I wrong!" H.P.

~ ❧ ~

"My husband died, and I was very lonesome. I had been dating someone for a very long time, and he would not commit. I met my ex, and we were married in less than a month. Later, I found out that he knew he was going to lose his job. He was very charming, but I would later learn that things he said were all lies." L.E.

~ ❧ ~

"I married the second time because I was lonesome; he was younger than I, and the marriage didn't work out because I hadn't known him long enough." F.A.

~ ❧ ~

"After my divorce, I was working in small towns all over the Midwest, and I never had any companionship away from work. I met a girl and married her to have a companion, but that didn't last long." W.O.

~ ❧ ~

"I wanted someone to spend time with, and I found someone who was convenient. We had known each other for some time since I used to cut his daughter's hair, and we were both divorced. We got to know each other better, and we were both lonely, living in empty houses, so we figured we would live under one house and get married. We did, but the marriage was boring—not as exciting as my first. It was more for companionship than anything else." M.A.

~ ❧ ~

"I married the second time because I was lonely and didn't want to spend the rest of my life alone. I was having problems making ends meet, supporting two kids on my own. This contributed to the hasty marriage as I foolishly thought the income from two is better than from one." D.N.

~ ❧ ~

"We married because we wanted to spend our lives together (so we thought). However, I think that sometimes people are not ready to remarry after a divorce. I believe that it is important to spend time alone, getting to know who you are. We married because we both feared being alone even though we were both in our early thirties. Looking back, that was crazy! People that young shouldn't fear being alone." T.K.

~ ❧ ~

"I was lonely, and he was a charmer. He was younger. I thought it was cool to have a younger man (boy) wanting me. We had a good sex life at first, and he knew how to say and do the right things. I wasn't in my right mind. I didn't pay attention to my heart and just went along for the ride. I didn't want to fail again so I stayed in it to try and make it work. That was wrong because it only got worse." A.J.

~ ❧ ~

"I was divorced, alone and lonely, when I met my brother's best friend from childhood again after not seeing him for thirty years. We fell into that 'it must be fate' scenario, and the relationship progressed even though serious warning bells were ringing loudly in my head. The warning bells were right; it didn't work out." E.F.

9
Wrong Reason #5
Romance Me, I'm Yours

❧ ❧ ❧

*The trouble with some women is that they
get all excited about nothing...and then
they marry him.*

Some people are suckers for romance. Unfortunately, we all know what happens to suckers. At the same time, you're not one bit wrong to want to find someone you can fall in love with and live with happily ever after. But it's not normal to be a love addict, to feel like you *have* to be in a relationship to feel alive and desirable. Are you one of the romance-driven? Will you marry someone because he or she romanced you and you love that being-romanced feeling?

Addicted to Love

Addiction means you are habitually or compulsively devoted to something. And, just like someone who has an addiction to drugs or alcohol, you may find being in love addictive. Perhaps you daydream of Prince Charming or Princess Gorgeous sweeping you off your feet. Most people assume this problem is more of a girl thing than a boy affliction, but, in truth, men are prey to the romance syndrome, too.

Some people simply can't stand being without a love interest. If you're one of the "in love with love" clan, you aren't happy unless you have someone to complete this fantasy for you. Everyone wants someone to love, to be with. We want someone to think we're great. But it's a *huge mistake to remarry when you've put the focus on love and not on the particular person offering it.* In the extreme, almost anyone will do if you're compulsively driven to find a love. The crux of the flawed premise here is that being madly in love with love renders you unable to see or think straight about another person. Your rose-colored glasses make everyone look wonderful. Basically, you don't give yourself a chance to evaluate a partner objectively as a marriage prospect. Signals of being addicted to love include these behavior patterns:

- You talk about the opposite sex constantly.
- You tell friends how your new love romanced you.
- You are dazed by the prospect of having a physical relationship with him or her.
- You act dreamy about the idea of getting married.
- If one person exits your life, you're immediately searching for his or her replacement.

How do you break an addiction? The first step is to acknowledge the problem. The second step is to be aware of the risks when you're exposed to your addiction. If you are a romanceaholic, admit it and be on guard when you're exposed to someone who triggers your romantic instincts. That way if you automatically think "marriage," you can shut yourself down.

Beware of Chasers

Have you ever had anyone pursue you with flattery? You hear the beguiling news that you're beautiful, handsome, fascinating, intelligent, gorgeous, charming, witty, a knockout. Of course, you've always suspected you were all of those things, but it's good to hear the truth verbalized, right? Chasers know the lure of well-tuned flattery that gets them where they want to go. They know how to reel you in with glowing love words, even though they just met you and hardly know you. The message the chaser sends is that he is smitten. He wants you and no other. Some chasers repeat this pattern because they are love addicts. Others do it because they have learned from experience that *this routine works.* If you're a love addict yourself, you can't help but interpret these dramatic proclamations as sure signs of love. It's hypnotic, and the love-speaker is irresistible. And you're especially vulnerable to a chaser if you haven't had someone in your life for some time. When this person blows your mind by telling you how deeply he is in love with you, how could you fail to follow suit and be in love? Again, the problem is that when you are blinded by love, you are blind.

Does Sex Really Equal Love?

We men sometimes confuse sexual appeal with love (some women do this, too). While men may not be as vulnerable as women to receiving flowers, romantic cards, and the like, we are very likely to think we have found the right one if we expect (or experience) the sex to be special. In the same way that some men have learned that romantic talk and actions can ensnare a woman, some women have learned that sex can close the deal with a man. In our interviews, we had many men say that sex motivated them to remarry, often overlooking potentially troubling issues. Sex can create love-blindness as much as any other romantic behavior.

Victor Couldn't Survive Without Sex

Victor was a 47-year-old man who had been married most of his adult life. His wife had fought cancer for three years, and she finally passed away, leaving Victor a lost and broken man. Most of all, he thought he was unable to survive without having sex. Victor had never had to go longer than a week or so without having sexual relations.

For the time his wife was ill, she had been unable to accommodate him. Now that he was widowed, he felt the need even more. But Victor had a problem. He didn't want to sleep with anyone outside of wedlock. He had taught his children that sex outside of marriage is wrong. His two grown daughters would disapprove, and the one teenage daughter who lived at home would be crushed if her father brought home women. Victor became a man with a mission to find a wife.

Tracy had never been married, but she always wanted to be. She had a long career of dating. Victor was a prime candidate. They met at a local event. The two desperate people began telling each other whatever the other wanted to hear. Tracy said she loved children and would be happy to help Victor raise his teenage daughter. She invited him to her apartment and told him that she, too, had strong sexual needs.

Victor proposed within two weeks of their meeting. Neither person knew anything about the other, but they learned quickly after the wedding. Tracy learned that Victor had apparently been having an affair with a married woman at work during the time of his wife's illness. This lady called him continually. His remarriage meant nothing to her. Also, the teenage daughter hated Tracy and made her life miserable. Likewise, Victor found out some surprises about Tracy. She had bouts of depression that never surfaced during the brief time they dated. The tension with the daughter brought them on in a big way. Victor learned the hard way that remarrying just to have a sexual relationship and demonstrate to his children that he would not "live in sin" proved disastrous.

Flattery Got His Foot in the Door

Jillian told us the story of her ill-fated remarriage and eventual divorce that started out when her boyfriend pursued her until she just couldn't say no. Darryl told her she was wonderful and the most beautiful woman he had ever seen. After two months, he asked her to marry him. A few months later, Darryl and Jillian were husband and wife. Unfortunately, Darryl turned out to be something of a nutcase. Jillian admitted that she had noticed many of his bizarre traits prior to marriage. When we asked why she made such a bad choice, she said that she didn't choose him, he chose her. She went on to say that that was the way it always worked with her. She would passively wait for someone to take an interest in her. When a man went after her aggressively, she went for it.

If you don't expose yourself to a variety of marriage candidates because you are not very willing to date, then you are expecting someone to choose you. And when that person does pursue you, you're in, no matter what. It is only by chance that this one person is a great mate for you. Why select from a sample of one? Waiting for a rider on a white horse is dangerous stuff. Make sure that when you're looking for your next spouse, you look carefully and choose with eyes wide open. Be the selective one. Don't passively wait to get chosen.

Let's Get Serious

Sybil was always in love with someone. Even in elementary school she had romantic fantasies about guys who didn't know she was around. By the time she was in high school, she was going steady. Playing the field didn't appeal to Sybil. She preferred to "get serious" with someone as soon as she could. When she found Walt, the boyfriend she wanted to marry, she smothered him with attention. At 18, she was married to him. By 22, she was divorced. Sybil said they really had nothing in common and that he paid little attention to her after the wedding. She admitted that this was not much different from how he acted when they were dating. She just thought he would be different after they were married or that she could change him.

A year after her divorce from Walt, Sybil met Don, who was older and more experienced. He was a smooth operator. Don took her to candlelight dinners, plays, and movies. He sent romantic cards and called her constantly. Their phone conversations were full of love talk. This was the man she had been searching for all of her life. But her friends pointed out some potential problems: Don had been married three times, and he'd left his last wife after only a year. Of course, he had reasonable explanations for everything. His last wife didn't appreciate and understand him. Another problem was that Don drank a lot of wine when they went to restaurants and clubs. Again, he explained that his doctor had urged him to have a couple of drinks every day to keep his cholesterol in check. The chase continued for a number of months. Sybil was battling with her parents about Don. They insisted that he was too old for her, that his previous marital life raised serious questions about his fidelity, and that he might be an alcoholic. Things got so bad that she broke off contact with her parents, hurting them in the process. Sybil just couldn't tolerate any negative feedback about Don. He obviously was very much in love with her and she with him, so how could a marriage based on great love and devotion fail? Sybil told naysayers that everyone has baggage. Why pick on Don just because he has had a difficult time finding the right woman? She was sure that with her, things would be different; he would be a committed husband.

You think you know the rest of the story, right? You may be surprised to hear how it spun out. One day Don suddenly disappeared. He didn't call. He didn't send flowers and notes. He just disappeared. Sybil never heard from him again. But she did eventually meet an associate of his, who told her that Don loved the chase, and would take it all the way up to the altar and then bolt, like in the movie *Runaway Bride*. Obviously, Don did go through with marrying occasionally, but he couldn't stick with it. Sybil was lucky. She had been prepared to remarry in spite of evidence of issues that could be marriage ending. If it were not for Don's disappearance, she would have said yes and no doubt lived to regret it.

What Went Wrong

Sybil allowed her romantic notions and love addiction to get in the way of her common sense and discernment. Insecure about herself after the first marriage failure, she was vulnerable to a man who assured her that she was a winner. Don chased her with words and deeds that said he thought she was wonderful. To Sybil, flattery was the same thing as love. Being in love or falling in love is not the same thing as truly loving someone. Anyone who has gone through a divorce knows how the early "in love" feeling can turn into falling out of love or worse. You may even come to hate the person you said you loved a few short years ago. Sybil's reaction to being swept off her feet was that she suspended good judgment to the point of rejecting and distancing her parents. When you're consumed by love, you want nothing to interfere, and you'll do anything to avoid breaking the spell. And that is just what it is—a spell. Your lover uses love to cast a spell on you so that you can't see him for who he really is. You see only what he wants you to see.

When you're in high school, people have looks, personalities, and little else. You choose a person to marry because he's handsome or popular. When you get a little or a lot older, particularly if you've been divorced, you realize that there are many issues to consider when you're thinking about marrying. Some of the things you should consider about your intended: Is he kind? Will she be faithful? Is he able to earn a living? Does she have addictions or bad habits? Will he accept your children? Are your families compatible? Clearly, you have to look at the other person with a rational eye before saying "I do." If you know you are a sucker for romance, be on guard. Don't allow yourself to fall for someone before really getting to know him. If you do get involved, and even if you come to your senses later, it will be painful to let him go.

Sybil was crushed when Don disappeared. She couldn't separate the fact that he had a serious problem from the impact it had on her ego. She had to tell her parents and friends that she had been dumped. This made her even more vulnerable to and skeptical of the next man who might come along. She was lucky that she didn't have a quickie marriage destined to fail, but she still suffered a high cost.

How Do You Define Love?

Examine how you define love. In the book *The Five Love Languages* by Dr. Gary Chapman, he suggests that different people define love in different ways. Some think that words of affirmation amount to love. Others interpret love to be when they receive gifts. Still others feel loved when they receive quality time, kind acts, or physical affection. If you're a person who defines love by the other person's romantic actions, be aware that there are people who feel and show love in different ways. Being open to these other people expands your options and prevents you from being as vulnerable to chasers.

Are You at Risk?

Are you a romanceaholic who is at risk for a remarriage mistake? Do you...

- always get dreamy about Prince Charming or Princess Gorgeous?
- find that you're always in love with someone or seriously looking?
- constantly talk about the opposite sex?
- believe you're in love whenever you expect great sex with someone?
- find flattery, love talk, and romantic actions irresistible?
- have a tendency to be swept off your feet?
- always want to "get serious" with your dates?

If several of these descriptions sound familiar, you're definitely in good company. Most of us want to be romanced and find that perfect mate. But lots of people have told us that their romantic natures gave them a serious case of love blindness. If that's you, here are some ideas for a cure.

Become a skeptic. We know this is easier said than done. You love having someone attracted to you, but even so, you can stay alert for red flags. When you're dating, keep a running tally of the questions you have about this person. Include possible issues you see that could become problematic.

Avoid chasers. You'll recognize them right away because they come on like gangbusters. The chaser will tell you that he has never met anyone in his life like you. Or she loves you and must have you or she will die. You get the picture. It's a good idea to ask others about the person's history. Was she this way with other men she had relationships with? Does he have a pattern of courting? Is she an actress in her reaction to you? Are you really that special or is it a routine?

Go slow. The biggest problem for romanceaholics is they want to rush in and lock in those wonderful feelings. You assume that the surest way to guarantee that you can continue to enjoy the love-fest is to get married. If you have this problem, vow that you won't marry someone for at least two years from the time you start dating that person. This will give you time to see what an ongoing relationship would be like and the opportunities to catalog any problems. Try not to "get serious" too quickly. Decide to take it one day at a time and just enjoy each other's company.

Look at love in your past relationships. In your marriage, how did you feel loved? List the things that signaled that the person loved you. Are there things besides displays of affection or sex? Recognize that there are many ways of showing love, and that deeper love takes time.

Open your mind and look at other things. When you exclusively focus on romance or sex (or any one thing), you ignore all the other qualities that are important in selecting a spouse. Begin compiling a list of the ideal traits you want in your next marriage partner. Expand your thinking. Include issues such as character and history.

After his failed marriages, Ed realized that what was important to him was not how someone looked or what she said or did, but how she made him feel. "If a woman was a phony, I could spot it in a hurry. Using this new criterion opened me to a lot of people I might have never considered before. In fact, my wife and I discussed prior to our marriage that we were not each other's 'type.' In hindsight, I saw that whenever I went for my 'type,' it never worked out."

Blinded by the Light

Romance is a double-edged sword. It makes everything look shiny, but, at the same time, that sparkle can blind you. Love, romance, and sex were three key words used in many of the divorce stories from the national survey Ed conducted. Not surprisingly, some people admitted they were hoodwinked because they *wanted to believe* and didn't question enough. Don't go love-blind when you pick your next spouse. Easier said then done, we know. But make it your goal.

"I was always in love with the idea of being married." H.N.

~ ❧ ~

"First time I was pregnant, ashamed, and thought I had no other choice but to marry. I was seventeen. We were married twenty-five years. The second time, I was blindsided by a man who was so romantic and so very generous. Truth was, he didn't know what he wanted and went on to the next woman after five years." D.K.

~ ❧ ~

"My ex was a smooth talker who was very romantic until after we married, and then he became very controlling and jealous. It was like he became a different person. He did not want me to have any friends or be with my family. He wanted me to work two jobs while he only worked part-time or did not work at all." A.R.

~ ❧ ~

"I was attracted to a very attractive lady who was very good in the area of sexual abilities, much more so than my ex-wife. It was the excitement that blurred my line of reason. This one came along, and like most will say, she was a once-in-a-lifetime opportunity, so I took it. Things changed after the marriage. She was somewhat of an actress." J.W.

~ ❧ ~

"I really didn't want to get married at this point, but I was swept off my feet by a younger man who romanced me with flowers, dinner, dancing, etc. He convinced me that I was getting older and he was the best I could do. I really liked the couple bit, so I thought it would work out. He had a good sense of humor and three out of four of my children liked him. Won't be so blind next time." L.F.

~ ❧ ~

"We had great sex and little else on which to have a lasting relationship. She was divorced from an overbearing and cruel man, was making minimum wage, and had a little girl who needed a dad." T.P.

~ ❧ ~

"I was dazzled by my husband's intellect and personality and wanted to hitch my wagon to his (perceived) star. He made all the right moves. At a vulnerable time in my life, I wanted to form a family with him, not seeing that he was also undergoing instability with the breakup of his first marriage." J.I.

~ ❧ ~

"I went to my twenty-year class reunion, and he just glommed on to me. For months he lied to me, but I was naïve and couldn't see it. He came to visit me, and I went once to visit him. Really, you have to watch a person in his environment to really know what he's like. Because it was long distance and because of the lies, I thought I was going into a relationship where someone would help me with the tasks that were hard or impossible for me to do. He immediately started poisoning me and eventually took all my money." I.F.

~ ❧ ~

"My second husband swept me off my feet with dinners, flowers, presents for me and my daughter, talk of loving and adoring me forever, etc. He was heavily involved in a self-help program but said definitely he would not expect me to join him in it. After we married, I found out almost everything he had said was a lie. I had been a single parent for seven years and felt that my daughter deserved a full-time father.

Before the marriage he treated her wonderfully. After we married, he was jealous of any time I spent with her and was extremely verbally abusive to both of us." B.V.

~ ❧ ~

"I re-met my childhood sweetheart after nearly thirty-five years, and everyone was so caught up in the 'romance' of it, that we just went along with it. Neither of us was the same person as we had been, and it was a disaster." J.K.

~ ❧ ~

"I thought that having great sex with the right person made her the right one. Found out that it was a mistake after all. All she really wanted was my name and money. What a fool I was!" K.T.

~ ❧ ~

"I was introduced to my last husband by family. Most of my close friends had their doubts, but I was so totally enamored by the attention that I failed to hear or see any warning signs until it was way too late. Looking back now, there were lots of things that should have set off warning flags, but didn't. I will be more careful in the future, that is for sure. The hormones are nice, but not for ruling the mind." E.S.

~ ❧ ~

"I married my last husband because I truly thought he worshipped the ground I walked on. We had not known each other closely for very long, even though we had worked together for a few years. He had never been married before, and I truly believed that he wanted to get away from his parents' home and thought that marriage was the best option. Too many romantic feelings can confuse you." M.H.

10
Wrong Reason #6
Jump-start My Life

❧ ❧ ❧

Are you bored?
Do you lack a real social life?
Are you lacking goals, dreams, and passions?
Is there something missing in your day-to-day existence?
Do you feel your life is on hold?
Then we have the answer for you:
Find someone and get married.

Just kidding! This may seem like a silly example but, unfortunately, many people feeling incomplete after their divorce solve their problem just this way. How does it happen?

Stalled in the Slow Lane

Why do we divorced people get stuck in the past? Why do we see no future? Why do we feel lost, bored, and aimless? When you are married, your future is well defined. You will be with your husband or wife until death do you part. You will raise your children together. You have some financial security with two possible breadwinners. You have mutual married friends and other family as a support system. You are set. And then, Boom! it all blows up. Now you have to start over, and everything is turned upside down.

We have seen a number of people in divorce recovery who have a "woe is me" outlook, a negative view on everything. These people have a laundry list of what their exes did wrong, and why their divorces have doomed them. They blame everyone else for their current circumstances. If you are totally focused on finding the guilty party in the divorce and dwelling on all the things in the past that went wrong, you can't move forward.

Another reason for being stuck is that you don't want to do the hard work. Yes, friends, growing through a divorce and building a new life for yourself is work. You have to learn and be willing to heal from the past, and that takes time. You have to construct a new social life for yourself. You have to solve financial problems that come with a split. You have to resolve how you will care for your children, and deal with the demands or lack of interest of your ex-spouse in this area. Life can be overwhelming, and it is often very trying. If you are not willing to make the effort, then you fall into a deep hole.

When you want someone else to pull you out of that hole, the problems begin. No one else can make you happy. *You* have the responsibility to make yourself happy. Put the shoe on the other foot: Would you want to marry someone who was perpetually miserable and her reason for marrying you was so you could fix her problems? Now you have the responsibility of making her happy. If you fail, you will hear about it. She will make you miserable along with her. When you look at it this way, you can see why it is a bad idea to remarry so that someone else can fix you, alleviate your boredom, make you happy, and jump-start your life. A marriage based on this motivation is dead on arrival because you have given your spouse an impossible mission. She will absolutely fail. You will be disappointed. Another divorce is likely. When you are feeling the need for someone else to complete you or make you happy, you are not ready to remarry.

Judy—Get a Life

Judy married Alan, her high school sweetheart. They had a wonderful marriage. Alan was an extrovert; Judy was an introvert.

Judy's main focus was her children and her extended family. She had four sisters and a brother. Most of their friends were Alan's friends he met through his work and hobbies. Judy had worked as a receptionist before they married, but gave that up to be a full-time housewife when the children were born. The couple traveled extensively. Alan made all the arrangements. Alan was a wonderful father and provider. Life seemed perfect for Judy. Then it all came crashing down 24 years after it started.

When the last child went off to college, the couple was alone in their home again. At first they were both excited about being able to spend more quality time together. However, they just never seemed to get the hang of being empty nesters. The problem, according to Alan, was "Judy was boring." She never had anything interesting to say. She never brought any new friends into the relationship. She sat around all day, and when Alan got home from work, she was so starved for attention that she smothered him. He wanted to unwind and relax. She wanted him to tell her about his whole day. They just didn't seem to have anything in common anymore. Their next step was marriage counseling. The counselor told Judy that she needed to develop her own life now that the children were gone and Alan was still working. She suggested that Judy join a women's group or take up a hobby. The counselor asked Alan to be patient and to help Judy adjust to these new circumstances. However, little changed over the next few months. Judy continued to lean on Alan for adult contact and stimulation. She became sullen and demanding. This had now gone on for almost three years. Their problems grew worse rather than better. The crash occurred when Alan told her he was leaving.

After the divorce, Judy fell into a depression, which she was unable to end. Judy felt like her life was over. She was bitter and angry at Alan, at their mutual friends who began to distance themselves from her, and even at her own family. Her negative attitude pushed people away. In our divorce recovery group, we ask people to work on forgiving their spouses and to begin developing a social network for themselves. Judy was stuck. She wouldn't forgive and blamed her ex-husband for her current circumstances. She didn't want to make any effort to meet new friends or become part of any singles group. When we asked her what goals she had for herself, she said she had none. In her mind, life was over. She was just subsisting.

Richard was in the same divorce recovery group, and he had a similar story, but with a twist. Richard decided he missed sowing some oats when he was younger so he left his wife. After a few months of being with as many women as he could, reality struck. He had made a *big* mistake. He begged his wife to take him back and admitted that he was a fool. She said emphatically, "No!" All this occurred before Richard came to our divorce recovery group. Once there, he glommed on to Judy, and she to him. These two were an emotional train wreck waiting to happen. They saw in each other a chance to solve their respective problems.

Richard and Judy began talking about getting married. They had all sorts of rationalizations about why they were perfect mates for each other. Richard even said he was now glad that his ex didn't take him back. Judy said she and Richard did exciting things that she never did with Alan. This was a match made in heaven. Their marriage lasted about 18 months. Just as before, Judy expected Richard to provide friends and fun. The pressure was too much for him.

Judy's unwillingness to establish any life for herself made her vulnerable to anyone who offered her a chance to jump-start her life. This pattern had started for her during her first marriage. She tried to build a life off the friends and interests of her husband. When he left, she had no life of her own. Judy put herself in a vulnerable position during her marriage to Alan. She expected him to be the only source of happiness for her. This is an unfair demand to place on anyone. It drove Alan out of their marriage and was one cause of the divorce. And then Judy married again, never allowing or taking the time and effort required to heal and get whole after the divorce. She stayed in a stuck position. Instead of creating an active social life for herself after the divorce, she just plugged in another guy to fill the void.

Richard was not much better. He dragged his misery into the new marriage. Richard made a mistake by sabotaging his first marriage with a midlife fling. Being rejected by his wife after he came crawling back put him into the same type of vulnerable position as Judy.

Can two people in crisis solve their problems by joining together? No. The only people who could solve their problems were the people themselves. Judy was unhappy because of specific deficiencies in her life—friends, activities, interests, a reason to live. Because her previous husband had filled those needs for her, she assumed the answer was to remarry and find someone else who would do it again. The fallacy in her thinking would have been obvious to her if she'd taken the time to realize she was a social dependent on Alan, which didn't work and caused a rift in their marriage.

The Lure of Excitement

Grant was a rather handsome, fortyish, high school teacher who didn't date for a long time after his divorce. His conservative nature led to what most would call a boring life. He told us about his ill-fated remarriage to Loraine.

Loraine was the mother of a child in his class. They met at one of the parent-teacher nights held at the school. In contrast to Grant, she was outgoing, talkative, charming, the life-of-the-party. Grant saw in her a chance to have an exciting life. I think subconsciously he somehow thought her people-friendly personality would rub off on him. When she asked him to be her escort to a charity event, the relationship began.

Loraine had a big social life in town, and she was frequently called upon to chair various club and charity events. At first this was very awkward for Grant. He wasn't used to meeting new people or making polite small talk. Once he adjusted, he began to like it. All this social activity was quite a contrast to his dreary, normal days of teaching and going home to study and prepare for the next day's classes. Loraine liked Grant's shy demeanor and passiveness because it allowed her to be the headliner and never get upstaged by her mate. After seven months, Grant asked her to marry him. She accepted.

After the wedding, everything changed. Loraine wanted Grant to spend less time with the kids at school and join her at more of her social functions. It became a battle of wills. The marriage lasted three years. The excitement that Grant originally saw turned into a life full of emotional high drama—never easy. As the couple drifted apart, their physical intimacy went with it. One day Loraine came home and told Grant she had been having an affair for the past few months with the head of one of her charity groups. She said that she and Grant were just too different, that it was frustratingly hard dragging him along in her social life.

Grant believed his dull life could be invigorated by the exciting Loraine. He hoped her nature would rub off on him and make him outgoing, too. The reverse occurred. Her nature stifled Grant, and he couldn't compete with her. He was always "Mr. Loraine." In contrast, Loraine had sought someone who wouldn't compete with her, but she got a man whose personality was dampened by her dominant nature. Grant's desire to jump-start his life failed because he was counting on a new spouse to do the heavy lifting. Instead, he should have gone out and developed a social life with compatible people on his own.

Start Me Up

No one else can jump-start your life and make you happy. If you have a hole that needs filling because of divorce, you need to do the hard work and fill it yourself. This will be discussed later in detail, but suffice it to say that the starting point is to assume responsibility for yourself. When you are divorced, you have to complete the healing and growth process on your own before jumping back into marriage with a new mate. When you do that successfully, you will not need another person to complete you, to make you whole, to fill you up, and to make you happy. That healing process requires focusing on the future and having forgiven your spouse so that he or she has no continuing hold on you. You need to develop a social network and a plan for your life with goals and aspirations. It's hard work but essential to having a successful remarriage.

Are You at Risk?

Boredom can be as troubling as loneliness. Someone who has

a very different lifestyle from your own can seem like an exciting marriage prospect. Are you at risk of this marriage mistake, or looking for an electrical charge to your drab existence? Do you…

- feel dependent on others for your joy?
- remain continually unhappy?
- blame your ex and others for your problems?
- have few close friends you can spend time with?
- rarely participate in fun activities?
- seem stuck in a divorce mindset?
- expect your life to be energized when you remarry?

If your life seems dull and unfulfilling, *you* need to find ways to revitalize it without counting on another spouse to solve this problem for you. Here are some ideas to get started.

Stop the pity party. If you feel stuck in your past life or just can't seem to stop feeling sorry for yourself, take steps to gain perspective. The problem is often lack of hope. Make an effort to be around positive people who have successfully emerged from their divorces. In our divorce recovery groups, stuck people find hope when they see others who are further down the road and are happy and active again.

Shift your focus away from your divorce. Buy a piggy bank and plan to dedicate the money put into it to charity. Every time you find yourself talking about or blaming your ex, put in a quarter, dollar, or whatever will be painful. You can't concentrate on creating a new life for yourself if you spend all your energy thinking about the old one.

Find a new circle of friends. When you get divorced, everything changes for you…but everyone around you still has the same routine. They have their same circle of friends, same activities, same spouses. So you have to "break in" to their routine or find a new circle of friends.

Identify the things you like to do, and try some new ones. Don't expect someone else to give you a life. Do it for yourself. Sometimes the difficult part is taking the first step. Look in the local newspaper and begin making a list of the various activities you could experience. Look for groups that you might join. If you go to one and don't like it, try something else.

Pull yourself out of any addictions you are using to mask your grief. In the national survey Ed conducted, some said they were so depressed and bored that they began overeating, or drinking, or taking prescription (or illegal) drugs. You cannot permanently solve any problems that way. If you are in that mode, get professional help.

"I married a Russian woman I met through the Internet. Thought something different and exciting might be enough. I was wrong. There was no sexual attraction." C.B.

~ ❧ ~

"She was different than most of the women I had dated. She was a little wild and crazy....Drank more than anyone I had been with. Lots of partying and people around all the time....This was a lifestyle I had never experienced....It was fun at first but soon became a real problem....The drinking and partying was all we had, and it was not enough for me....I tried to get her to go to counseling, but she declined so we divorced after 18 months of marriage." V.S.

~ ❧ ~

"I married my ex-wife to fulfill my life. My codependency made me feel that I needed others to give my life worth." G.P.

~ ❧ ~

"I was bored and getting drunk to cover my miseries. Needed someone to pull me out of it and give me something to look forward to." R.O.

~ ❧ ~

"I married my second husband after knowing him for 8 or 9 months. I was divorced for 20 years and raised two sons alone. Dating him was like a whirlwind for me—he was exciting, and we did things I never experienced before. My life suddenly seemed so full. So when we fell in love, we got married soon after. Was married for only 3 yrs. 5 mos. when he left me and left behind thousands of dollars of debt, which I am paying off now. He didn't have a regular job, and I am employed full time. He ruined my life and he realized it, so he decided to leave before things (financially) got worse." T.B.

"My mom and dad have been married for over 63 years. I have been married 6 times, and always because I am, was, and always will be in the mindset that I would like to have someone to share my life with and to be with to make the job of living easier. I'm always bored when I'm alone. Now, toward the end of my life, I find that I have made it through life and still have no one to share it with but the people who are taking this survey. Guess it just proves that life is not as we expect it to be. Have never found a wife who was true and did not cheat on me. I have never, not once, cheated and have always been a good provider. Just cannot pick the right one, that is all." D.P.

11
Wrong Reason #7
Feelin' the Pressure

❧ ❧ ❧

*I never knew what real happiness was
until I got married. Then it was too late.*

Is there anyone else who has an interest in whether you remarry or not? Maybe your parents want grandchildren or think you were happier when you were married. Some friends really like the person you're dating—think she (or he) is the right one for you and feel you need a little push. Your counselor keeps telling you that you should trust again and not be afraid to commit. Everyone tells you just because your first marriage led to a painful divorce doesn't mean it will happen again. "Stop stalling. He (or she) is the right person for you. Go for it!"

Have you heard words like these? Family, friends, and counselors want you to be happy. They have your best interest at heart. They want you to be happily married. Everybody wants you to marry Mr. or Ms. X, whom you have dated for some time. They "encourage you" whether you are ready to remarry or not. They have a stake in the game.

Get Back to "Normality"

Why do we experience pressure from others to remarry? Married people generally believe that marriage is the "normal" state, and they cannot envision how an unmarried person would want to stay that way for any length of time. These people love you, so their goal is to help you get back to normality. Family members may have their own hidden agendas. They may want to have grandchildren, and they need you to get married to legitimately make this happen. They may like the person you are dating and feel sorry for her (or him) that you have been stringing her along. They may want you to stop running around and living in sin. If your beliefs are the same, you may feel pressure to marry from your church, your family, your friends, or your own conscience. Your counselor believes he is supposed to help you make decisions when you are fearful or uncertain, and he may exert subtle or obvious pressure. And then there is the pressure from the person you are dating. She (or he) wants to get married and not be seen as a fool who just keeps waiting for you to pop the question.

Then there is pressure from society. Our culture supports the notion that single people are second-class citizens. The tax code discriminates against single people since those who are married get a tax break. Many married friends dropped you like a hot potato when you got a divorce. You may suddenly have become a threat to their marriages. They may fear that their spouses will now leave them, too, when they see that you had the guts to leave or that you are having so much fun. Or they may feel threatened by you. You are a beautiful, single woman, and husbands might now show interest. Married coworkers now feel sorry for you. They treat you like a lost sheep who needs help. They want to find the right match for you. All this matchmaking effort reflects the underlying belief that being single is undesirable and not normal.

What is wrong with people trying to help you find dates? What is wrong with family and friends encouraging you to get up the courage to ask or say yes to your love interest about marrying? What is wrong when the person in your life wants to be with you permanently? Nothing! The problem is when *you know* that something is wrong, and a little voice is telling you not to marry that person. If you are in a weakened state from your divorce, you might just say yes because of the pressure.

Remarrying Under Pressure

There may be a number of reasons that you should not remarry, at least not at this time or to this person. If you let outside influences get to you, you may regret it.

You're Not Ready

After divorce, everyone needs a reasonable period of time to heal and to grow. During this period you will need to become whole again with a full life *of your own.* This process takes varying amounts of time for different people. For most people it takes at least two years. For some, a lot longer. If you remarry sooner, you drag your unresolved issues and mess into your next marriage. Some people are instinctively good judges about whether they are ready to remarry. Others aren't so good. So be careful if "well meaning" people are pushing you along.

You Know the Other Person Is Not Ready

Have you ever dated someone you knew was just not ready to marry? He may be fragile from his previous marriage. She may still be sorting out issues with her children. He may be in the thick of battle with his ex over money or custody rights. She may be in a state of confusion or pain or anger. Whatever the reasons, you know he is not ready to remarry no matter what he thinks. She may want you to solve her problems by having you become an instant spouse replacement. He may put untold pressure on you. But you know better—especially after reading this book!

You Know the Other Person Is Wrong for You

Another mistake that can come about from external pressure

is where the woman (or man) you are dating is not the right one for you, but you weaken and marry anyway. Disaster. Now you might be asking: "Why would someone date the wrong person for any extended period of time?" The answer: Some people date the wrong person for years because it is easy or convenient. Dating can be hard for many divorced people. If you find someone to be with, you may just settle. But you know deep down he (or she) isn't the right person for you.

Here is another reason why some people stay involved with the wrong person for years: He is not a threat! You don't really want to get married yet, and you choose someone to date whom you know is not a real marriage prospect or will not pressure you. In effect, injured divorced people sometimes pick a transition person to "tide them over" until they are ready to remarry. Then they go out and search for the right one. This sounds a bit cruel, but it happens. In many of these cases, both parties are using each other because they don't want to commit beyond what they give to each other. Some even move in together knowing they will eventually split. When you allow yourself to get involved long-term with a person who is not a good marriage prospect, you run three risks:

- You will either stay in a relationship that is fulfilling in a very limited way.
- You will eventually have a painful breakup.
- You will succumb to pressure and marry for the wrong reason and suffer the consequences.

You Know You Are Wrong for the Other Person

This is a little unusual, but sometimes marriage is wrong when you know you are wrong for the one you are dating. It takes a brave and caring person to tell someone that you know yourself and you are not the best one for him. Ed recalls dating a woman who was very religious. Nothing wrong with that, except it was not his religion. "At the time I knew I would not care. However, I knew she would grow to be unhappy with me over time if we married. We had few shared histories or beliefs. This was bound to become a problem if we were married and had children. She didn't care at that stage. She said she was in love with me. Having been married before, I knew reality sets in not too long after the wedding bells chime. I knew I was the wrong person for her. The pressure she exerted on me to marry would have come back to bite her—and me."

Do You Buckle or Rebel?

One other note about pressure. How do you react to it? Are you a person who buckles under when your parents and friends incessantly bug you to do something? Or are you a person who rebels when you have pressure? Some respond in reverse when others tell them what to do. If they insist you break off your relationship with Ms. X, you may marry her to spite them. Obviously, the right way to handle pressure is to consider others' opinions because there may be some merit in what they are saying. But then use your own best judgment, and don't cave in to making decisions that run counter to your instincts and reasoning.

Buzz Dropped the Bomb

Doreen and her husband grew apart after an 11-year marriage. They separated amicably. Since there were no hostilities and the partners had had much time during the marriage to drift, Doreen adjusted well to the divorce. She told me that she had grieved for the past three years and that when the divorce was final, it was a nonevent. Doreen had little interest in dating, and she spent most of her time with work and hobbies. Doreen worked for a large food company as an accountant. An outgoing individual, she had many women friends at work who frequently invited her to join them for dinner or movies.

Three years after the divorce, a fellow employee introduced her to Buzz, an auditor who came to the company once a year. Buzz began an active courtship. Maybe I should say he pursued her passionately. Doreen spent increasing amounts of time with Buzz, but she told her friends that she was not in love with him. Nothing

Buzz did fazed Doreen, even his pleading proposals of marriage. She remained interested but not committed to anything beyond regular dating. Buzz began to enlist her friends to convince her that he was a great catch and that she should give in. Even Doreen's mother got into the act and told Doreen she wasn't getting any younger and that Buzz was the best she was going to do. Still nothing changed with Doreen.

One night Buzz dropped the bomb. He wasn't going to continue with Doreen unless she was going to marry him. They had now been dating almost five years. Doreen said no. After the breakup, family and friends started a full-court press telling Doreen she was a fool, that Buzz was perfect for her, and that everyone was angry with her given the way she led Buzz on. Doreen finally gave in and agreed to the marriage. She said she did so in spite of her better judgment. *Maybe those people are right.* So many thought he was the best one for her. After the wedding, Buzz changed dramatically. He was like Jekyll & Hyde. He suddenly stopped showing all the attention he once did while they were courting. This marriage was not going to work.

Doreen was a rather well-adjusted person except when it came to men. She refused to date or let herself have the experience of seeing what a range of men were like so that she could determine who she might consider remarrying. You might argue that Doreen was okay without any men. That seemed to be true, but having dated only Buzz put her in the awkward position of having no choices. She had the correct instincts to see that Buzz was not the person she should marry. Her family and friends had other ideas, and she weakened because of her lack of options and exposure to other prospects. Even before the wedding, she acknowledged that she had reservations, but her thinking was clouded by the pressure of so many people.

The Transition Woman

Jerrod got married at age 18 and divorced three months later. Now at the ripe old age of 21, he was divorced and glad of it. The marriage had been terrible, he said, and he never wanted to make that mistake again. In fact, he said he envied his uncle who was in his sixties and had never been married. This guy was cool. He had money, freedom, and women. For the next three years, Jerrod saw a lot of women but had few repeat dates. That got old.

Then he met Britney. She was a few years older and had been divorced some years before. Britney was a Christian, but also a desperate woman. They moved in together. To everyone who knew them, they seemed to be a great couple. They went everywhere together, had much in common, and looked the perfect match. Three years later, nothing changed. Six years later, nothing changed. Nine years later, nothing changed. Jerrod never asked Britney to marry him, and she never brought up the subject. The situation seemed in equilibrium. Then out of the blue, Jerrod asked her to move out.

Britney was crushed. She didn't understand this at all. How could he think this way after all the time they had been together? She insisted that he was just afraid of commitment because of the trauma from his first divorce. She demanded that he go with her to counseling.

The psychologist asked Jerrod to review his childhood and the details of his first marriage. After reviewing this, she told Jerrod that he needed to learn to commit. Look at his past. He skipped out on his first marriage and then refused to commit to Britney for nine years. She told Jerrod that he had a problem. She said marrying Britney was a way to prove to himself that he could have a serious, committed relationship. If he backed out now, he would just repeat this pattern over and over. Jerrod was distraught with the prospect that his life could be a series of failed relationships. He agreed to marry Britney. Once married, he was not like the person she had lived with. He was pensive and sullen. The marriage ended within the year. Jerrod told me he had made a mistake. Inside he knew Britney was not the right person for him. Their relationship had filled a need, but when he wanted out, he was looking for something more serious. Britney had turned out to be the one in transition. Jerrod has since married again, and has been happily so for more than 11 years.

Jerrod never learned anything from his divorce except, "Don't do that again!" Instead, he chose to attach himself to no one by dating different people every night. When he tired of this, he found someone who was willing to settle for a "no commitment" pledge of playing house. Britney was obviously so insecure that she compromised her moral values and was unable to demand what she wanted. She settled for this situation for nine years. If she had been demanding earlier, they probably would have broken up, but she would have learned where she stood years earlier. The fiasco marriage was the result of Jerrod's being analyzed and directed by a counselor who thought she understood her client, but she really didn't. Jerrod and Britney paid the price.

Listen to Your Gut

If you have an inkling that you are not ready to remarry, or that the other person is not ready, or that the person is not the right one for you, *don't do it!* No matter what others tell you. No matter how your partner begs and pleads. No matter what advice family and friends give you. No matter what "wise" counselors say. If you have reservations, wait. Allow yourself time to detect what is happening. Some people are gun shy and need a little push to take another chance in marriage. But more often than not, if you are pushed into marriage, it will backfire eventually.

Are You at Risk?

Amazingly, a variety of people have an interest in whether you get remarried. Listening to other people's advice is wise because they might see something you don't. However, *you* are the one who has to live with the consequences if you make a marriage mistake. Be on guard not to do anything against your better judgment, no matter how intense the pressure.

Do you...

- feel you are not ready to marry—for any reason?
- know the person you are dating is not ready to marry?
- have significant doubts about someone you are dating?

- know you are not the right person for someone you are dating?
- have people telling you that you will be happy if only you'll get married?
- believe that marriage is the only "normal" state?
- hear family or friends tell you they don't understand why you don't marry so and so?
- get moral advice from people suggesting quick marriages?
- have a fiancé or "significant other" who gives you ultimatums or reasons to marry him or her?

Then welcome to the club of those feeling the pressure to remarry. As you saw in the stories in this chapter, if you go against your instincts and let others drive you to marry, it usually doesn't work out. Here are some tips for handling the situation.

Give yourself more time or break it off. If you have some apprehensions and need more time to determine whether problems may be insurmountable, take the time. If, however, you know this relationship won't work, get up the gumption to break it off. Because breaking up is hard to do, some people find it easier to just get married. But remember how painful your divorce was. Do you want to risk going through that again if you know the odds are against you now? Reread some of the stories of people in this book and realize the cost they paid for ignoring their better judgment.

Kindly tell family and friends to mind their own business. The way we suggest doing this is simply saying, "I appreciate your interest in my welfare, but I have to decide what is best for me. Right now I am not ready to marry."

Tell the person you're dating the truth. If you have concerns and believe marriage is unlikely, don't string him (or her) along. You have an obligation to tell him kindly the truth. If this discourages him and he chooses to break off the relationship, that is his right. He may attempt to convince you otherwise about your concerns—"I will stop drinking," "I will never yell at you again," "How could you think that about me? I haven't been unfaithful," and so forth. Don't weaken if you have reason for your caution. Note in the "Can You Relate" stories at the end of each chapter how people believed the promises that fiancés made because they *wanted* to believe them, often to their detriment. Talk is cheap; wait to see the actions.

"I was tired of living with my intended, and my neighbor challenged me to get married…that's it." N.S.

"I was in a very vulnerable state due to a great loss I was grieving over. This person was desperate to marry, was putting a lot of pressure on." K.H.

"Met a man through my parents and my brothers (this was my second marriage). Was more or less pushed into this marriage by parents and brothers. They thought he would be able to take care of my three children and myself. For the first year everything was fine, than the dark side of him started showing through. He turned out to be a thief and liar. He would steal from companies and from family and friends. I could not believe he could be the way he was. He would buy me Christmas gifts, and they would disappear. He had taken them back for the cash. In other words, he was stealing from me. Quit my job and kicked him to the curb. The only thing I was thankful for was we did not have any children." E.C.

"Left a bad marriage and met a young woman. We moved in together, then after a short time of being together she pressured me to marry her or she would leave. I married, then she began her endless shopping. Convinced me to adopt, then left after getting the baby. Leaving me with the child." D.L.

"We dated for about a year and split up because it didn't work. Then he started sending me flowers & gifts. So I started seeing him again. We started living together. After about a year of living together I got pregnant. His family pressured me into marrying him (for the baby) & that his poor grandmother would die of a heart attack having a bastard grandchild. A month before my son was born, I gave in & got married even though the relationship wasn't working. In fact, I wore black to the wedding. Well the marriage lasted about 2 years & then it took me another 2 years to get the divorce finalized. During the divorce he stalked us. So I ended up moving 2 states away." P.M.

~ ❧ ~

"My father was dying and asked my ex to marry me so he would know I was being taken care of. I really didn't want to get married, but my father was worried I would be lost without him. It was his last wish, and I felt I had to do this for him. My father died two days after I got married. I was lost without him, and my life fell apart that very day. A word to the wise: Even on a deathbed, don't give them their last wish. My ex beat me and my children after my father died. So he changed a lot when he knew my dad wasn't there to see what he was really all about. But I know my dad saw from above, and my ex will pay for his ways." A.F.

~ ❧ ~

"We hadn't known each other long. He loved me, but I didn't love him. He threatened to kill himself if I didn't marry him, and I felt very sorry for him. The marriage lasted only a very short time. Even though he was very good to me, I just didn't love him. We were both on the rebound." M.C.

~ ❧ ~

"He kept pressuring me to get married because we had been living together for over a year and he wanted to make it legal. I was not ready for remarrying but was tired of hearing that he was ready." D.D.

~ ❦ ~

"I was pregnant and knew that my ex-husband would be a good father and husband, but I also knew that I was not in love with him. I should not have married him. Were we not expecting a baby, we both admit we probably would not have gotten married." T.O.

~ ❦ ~

"My mother had cancer and I was off work taking care of her. My boyfriend started saying it would be better if we were married for tax and insurance purposes. I felt since he was supporting the household at the time that I needed to do whatever I could do to help financially. He thought marriage was the answer—it was not. We are still 'friends' but not near as close as we would have been had we never married." F.K.

~ ❦ ~

"I met this friend from work who started helping me with things around the house, mowing, etc. Then his apartment burned down, so he moved in with me and the kids. He was my best friend. But I really didn't want to rush into anything at that point. My parents were very strict: What did the neighbors think, what are you teaching your kids, etc., guilt and pressure. So finally I said let's do it. He was so excited, but I knew walking down that aisle that this was a mistake." P.Q.

~ ❦ ~

"I was married twice. I got married the second time primarily because she was pregnant and I wanted my son to have a father around. Our marriage was okay to start and slowly went downhill. I tried to make it work, but just seemed it was not happening. We had differences but mostly seemed that the romance stopped. I believe that

I was not ready to get married again, but felt compelled to do so for my son." C.D.

"We had an affair while his wife was out of town. When she returned I told him I wouldn't be 'on the side,' which meant it was over. He misunderstood and left her without discussing it with me. Just showed up on my doorstep with all his things in the back of his truck. I felt responsible." L.A.

12
Wrong Reason #8
It's Time

❧ ❧ ❧

A woman ran an ad in the classifieds:
"Husband wanted." Next day she received
a hundred letters. They all said the same thing:
You can have mine.

Ding! What was that bell, you ask? It was a wedding bell going off in some divorced person's head telling him, "It's time." Time for what? It's time to marry. You wouldn't believe how many people have told us this story about first-time marriages and remarriages! All of a sudden a person decides he is ready to hear wedding bells. People hear this bell in their heads even if they have no partner in mind!

If this happens to you, there's trouble ahead. Your marriage vulnerability index just shot through the roof. You are suddenly motivated to get married. You become a man with a mission, a woman with a will, a person with a purpose. In this condition, a clear perspective on any bride- or bridegroom-to-be goes out the window. "Don't waste time getting to know the other person; it's time to marry. So let's get on with it." If this sounds extreme, you would be surprised what a motivator this can be. Why would anyone suddenly have the urge to merge? In our research, we found there are lots of reasons, ranging from feeling left out among married friends to the ticking biological clock. This bell dings in the heads of both men and women.

Someone's Going to Become Mrs. Rocky

Rocky was normally a very sound and mature individual. We say normally because some years back, he lost his way and behaved like a zombie with a fried brain. After a sour marriage in his twenties, he dated around and just had fun. All of his married friends were jealous. He seemed to be carefree. He had plenty of money. He had no shortage of gorgeous women to escort. Then Rocky turned 35. The gong went off in his head, and the blast blew out his mind. It was like an oven timer that couldn't be turned off. It just kept ringing and had to be dealt with.

One night at dinner with Ed and some other friends, Rocky told us, "It's time." Yes, those were his exact words. Everyone said, "Time for what?" He said it was time to marry. So we asked, "Who is the lucky woman?" To our surprise he said he didn't know; he didn't exactly have a prime candidate ready; he couldn't fill in the blank with a name. Some as-yet-unnamed woman was soon going to become Mrs. Rocky. This sounded crazy, dangerous, foolish, mad. Our worst fears were confirmed when he met Jan a few months later. He now had a name to go in that blank. He had already talked with her about getting married.

Here's the rest of the story about Rocky told by Ed:

> He introduced me to Jan at a restaurant where a number of us met for dinner. I brought along a book for him to read that was a bestseller at the time. When I handed it to him, Jan went into a tailspin. She told me she was a marriage counselor by profession, and she didn't want Rocky reading that book. I was shocked. She got so upset she began crying and had to depart for the ladies' restroom. Needless to say, I later tried to talk Rocky out

of even considering marrying Jan. How could someone as independent and carefree as Rocky be able to get along with such a controlling woman? But it was all for naught. The bell in his head had rung, and he was going to hear it at the altar. Years after their divorce was final, we discussed that evening. I said to Rocky, "You knew this was not going to work. I told you so and so did others. Why did you do it anyway?" He admitted, "When it's time, it's time, and you have to go with it." He said all of his friends had married or remarried. He was feeling old. He wanted to settle down again, be married again. He wanted to prove he could be "normal" like everyone else. He rationalized all the good qualities his fiancée had in order to overlook the problems that were in his face at the time. "So it wasn't really about love?" I asked. No, he hadn't had time to find out if he really loved her. In fact, he recalled that he didn't even feel that much attraction to her. When it's time, it's time.

Rocky was set up by his time clock. Once the bell rung, he refused to fight. Can we really blame Jan for the divorce? When the divorce papers were filed, both parties could blame each other. He was a little too irresponsible, too carefree. She was too controlling. Not a good combination. All that was blatantly obvious upfront…obvious to everyone but them, that is. The two marriage prospects went deaf, dumb, and blind to all their faults. Only years later could they even admit what happened.

Biology Trumps Logic

Ginger had a rough marriage. She confided that her husband had begun to drink heavily during their marriage, something she never recognized when they dated. Oh, he drank a lot of beer when they would go out. She just didn't put two and two together. She was in our divorce recovery group because she had divorced him, and she wanted to "recover" as quickly as possible.

In her mid-thirties, Ginger had a goal in mind: to have a baby. She always wanted to have children. Most of her friends now were married with kids. But there was a problem. She had tried everything to get her husband to stop drinking, to attend AA, to stop being in denial. He had made continual promises. He had quit for a time. He begged her to understand him. In reality, she had done everything she knew how to do, including being patient. Her patience had run out because her biological clock had bonged in her head: "Get on with it before it's too late," it said. She didn't want this man to be the father of her children. That's why she divorced him.

The problem was her urgency in finding that next sperm donor. That's the reality of how she looked at it. She was actively seeking someone to impregnate her. There's nothing wrong with wanting children. Most men could accommodate the need she had. But most men would not make an appropriate husband for Ginger. She was on a dangerous mission, and there seemed no way to stop her. Logic is useless against unfettered obsessiveness about biology.

Rob turned out to be the unlucky victim. He was a low-key guy who dated very little. On their first date, Ginger raised the issue of having children and asked his views. He was open to it, but it wasn't an instant priority. Because Ginger decided early that Rob was "the one," she had a plan to close the deal. She went all out—cooking for him, overwhelming him with words of affection, bringing him little presents, and attacking him like a cat in heat. She told us there was no way he was going to get away. And he didn't. Ginger got pregnant, and Rob married her four months before the baby was born.

We learned much later from Ginger that it hadn't really worked out like she had planned. She got the baby all right. In fact, two of them. Rob turned out to be a very dependent person. He was as much a child as the infant. He was always needy and never would do anything to help around the house. We don't know what finally happened to their marriage. We do know it probably wasn't good.

Ginger's desire to escape a marriage ruined by alcohol was understandable. Her desire to marry a man free of addiction to father her children was sensible. Her desire to have children before she reached her forties was logical. What wasn't smart was the mad dash to find a sperm source who might (by chance) also be an appropriate husband. Like the old saying goes, "Marry in haste, repent in leisure."

Are You at Risk?

Clocks tick. We get older. Biology can trump logic. This is a very common and also very difficult situation to overcome. If you suddenly feel the need to remarry, pull up the reins—especially if you have no ideal candidate in mind. If you believe "it's time" to get remarried, you may be at great risk. You may become far less selective than you would normally be and grab anyone available to make it happen. When you decide it's time, convincing yourself otherwise will be difficult. So don't treat this problem lightly. Are you at risk for this behavior? Do you...

- hear wedding bells going off in your head?
- feel your biological clock ticking and you're in the thirteenth hour?
- have friends who are all married or remarried, and you feel left behind?
- think seriously about remarrying and don't even have a real prospect?

Don't ignore these symptoms! You can see from the stories in this chapter how people ruined a part of their lives by allowing their chronological or biological impulses to tie the knot with anyone available. Here are some tips you can do to reverse course.

Recognize the situation you are in. You can't stop yourself from heading over the cliff if you are in denial. Weigh the risks of a quick marriage to satisfy the bells ringing in your head against the potential outcome of another painful divorce. If you feel your remarriage vulnerability index is high, make the conscious decision to do nothing. Give yourself a long window of time in which you agree upfront that you will not remarry. Wait until these chronological and biological urges subside.

When you feel like anybody will do, don't do anything with anybody. Allow enough time to come to your senses before letting these circumstances, which are the wrong reasons to remarry, dictate your actions. Don't date at all for a time.

Halt any mission to marry that you have undertaken. If you sense you are on a mission to marry because of a feeling that it's time, be conscious of your situation. Call off the pursuit.

Be extra careful in screening any marriage prospects. Don't suspend your good judgment. Make a list of red flags that could be a problem with the person you're dating. Like with any physical ailment you have, get a second opinion. Ask friends to help you evaluate anyone you date. The idea here is to be aware of your vulnerability to overlook glaring problems just to make a marriage happen.

"Thought I was in love, and it was time to get married. Intuition said not to do it the couple of weeks leading up to the wedding. I didn't trust my feelings and realize what my intuition was trying to tell me. Knew *for sure* it was a mistake while on my honeymoon, but then it was too late." J.F.

~ ❦ ~

"My ex-husband decided it was time to settle down and get married after he got back from serving in the army. He went through his list of old girlfriends, and I was the first one available. We had dated in high school, and I had been crazy about him right from the start. I considered him my first love." K.G.

~ ❦ ~

"I fell in love with him…and we started living together too quickly. Also, my first husband didn't want children and I did…so I was hoping to have a baby by my second husband. My time clock was ticking." P.T.

~ ❦ ~

"I remarried because I thought it was time as I had been single for a number of years. I truly liked the person I married, but I didn't love him. I thought it would be nice for my boys and it wasn't. He had no interest in them or his daughter from a previous marriage. His main interest, I found out, was himself." G.S.

~ ❦ ~

"I have asked myself this question a million times, and for sure I don't know why I remarried him! Still, I think that for one thing, that biological clock must have been ticking really loud, and I thought I could be a better mother if I tried it again. Then, too, I had grown tired of always being the one to sit down every month and pay the bills. Lots of little things like that. I had been through a lot of relationships that hadn't really gone anywhere. I thought he was intellectual and maybe there would be room for intellectually stimulating conversation. That never developed. But like I said, I think we got married too fast and didn't really know each other." F.O.

"We just thought, hey, let's do it. We had been going out for a year and figured it was time. She turned out to be a monster after the wedding." S.H.

"I was 43 yrs. old, making $75,000/YR. Thought my clock was running out and needed to have the house, car, 401(k), and a husband to grow old with or it would be too late. I just wanted companionship and a plan for old age....He insisted we should marry. He was Jewish, I was not. Bad idea! Turns out this guy was on Zoloft, had threatened suicide, and was a secret hater of women. Not a word from any of the family (his) about all this until the separation. I ended up with Post Traumatic Stress Disorder and broke! Men like my ex have dreams to control strong, successful women like me. And he did it—broke my spirit and moved on with my money and jewelry to a woman who has more money and dumped her three kids and a husband for him." V.M.

13

Wrong Reason #9
A Fish on the Line

✻ ✻ ✻

Why do older people get remarried?
Because they have a poor memory.

Let's say you've dated someone for a long time. Is it easier to break up or to get married? Amazingly, some people find it more comfortable to move forward into a "mistake marriage" than to back off and admit their relationship isn't working. This avoids the emotional turmoil and recriminations. It is passive! For the unproactive, marrying a bird in the hand happens early and often. Not a great way to choose a life partner, but you may have a tendency to slide right into home base without giving it much thought. Only later, when you begin to feel smothered by the reality of a marriage that shouldn't have happened, do you decide to back off and disconnect.

Breaking Up Is Hard to Do

Breaking up is hard to do is a song and a fact. We all hate

disappointing someone, especially when we've spent quality time together, shared intimacies, enjoyed laughter and play, and talked about our day's wrap-ups time after time. If you've been in a relationship, you know how difficult it is to end it. When you have deep feelings for someone, a split can be as painful as divorce. Furthermore, if you live with your mate, you share some of the issues of an actual divorce when you decide to go your separate ways. You have to divide the property you accumulated together. Parents, children, and other family are torn by the breakup. You have to begin your life over in new surroundings. Breaking up is a difficult decision and a stressful effort to undertake. And that's exactly why some people just don't do it, even when they should. One way to keep from facing a breakup is to stay in the relationship way past the time when it's fulfilling. Another is to get married rather than endure the agony of splitting.

Going to the Chapel

In our research on people who remarry when they should be breaking off a relationship, we have found a variety of reasons this occurs. These are some of the most common.

You think you won't get another chance. Depending on your age and level of self-confidence, you may figure that you should jump on this opportunity to marry because it could be your only chance. Your stream of thought tells you, "Okay, I have a live one whom I know (the good and the bad), and if I don't marry her, I won't have another chance. Who else would have me? I've put on weight. I've developed some bad habits. I'm set in my ways. I might as well ride the horse I came in on."

You think you can't do any better. You realize that you've dated quite a few people, and most of them are losers. You figure that you know this person, even though he has a lot of faults, and you two fight constantly, and you're miserable most of the time. But you're almost positive you can't do any better. Settling for a given (the one you're with) is better than taking a risk on finding someone else.

You fear that someone else will snap her up. You don't really like the person you're with, and you have nothing in common. But your friends are envious that you attracted someone so good-looking. If you let this person go, someone else is sure to grab her. You can't stand the thought of someone else getting her.

You think it's the right thing to do. You've been with this person so long that you just don't feel right about backing away and leaving. In fact, the idea seems awful to you—and wrong. Your ethical standards tell you that you're a better person than that. Marrying is the right thing to do.

You think you owe this person. You're thinking like this: "I have been with him so long now. How can I just back out and leave? That would be awful. After all this time, I have an obligation here. I owe this person the right to be married."

You're sure that a split sounds like too much trouble. You keep thinking about all the hassle involved in splitting up. Fighting over stuff. Handling the disapproval of friends who don't want you to break up. Disappointing your partner's parents who love you. Disappointing your family. Worst of all, you can't bear the thought of having to start over. You would have to date and find someone else, and the upshot could be that you would feel conflicted all over again. Who knows the future? It's just simpler to stay with the one you're with.

You think your relationship will be better when you're married. Yes, things are a mess now. But you suspect that's because you haven't made a commitment, and if you agree to marry, things will get better. Your partner keeps telling you that your problems will disappear once the two of you know that you can count on each other. After you become husband and wife, you'll iron out your differences.

Slip Out the Back or Hang Around?

Sometimes people decide to remarry just because they can. You may feel you're obligated to take the relationship "to another level." Or you may reason that getting married sounds easier than the trauma of breaking up. Whatever the situation, if the relationship is having *mucho problemas,* don't count on marriage to fix them. Maybe you're gambling that you can stay together as a married couple, and divorcing couldn't be that much worse than separating now. You may be hopeful when all the evidence points to no reason at all for optimism about this relationship.

Breakups are tough. But separating as two single people is infinitely easier than separating as a married couple. Divorces get the courts and the lawyers involved. Plus, you have money issues that your state has some say about. If you have children, legal entities will tell you what you can and can't do. And the emotional trauma of divorce is harder than splitting from a "boyfriend" or "girlfriend." So think twice before remarrying for the reason of simple lethargy. If the relationship won't work, you accomplish nothing by making things more complicated with wedding papers. You face payback time either now or later. You won't find an easy way out. Better to bite the bullet up front.

To help you summon up the courage you need to split when you know you should, consider these stories of a few people who did go ahead with an iffy marriage.

Doug Didn't Want to Do It

At 32, Doug was already a two-timer. To say that he was gun shy about remarriage is an understatement. In his first marriage, he found his wife in bed with a service technician—an ego blow of startling proportions. His second wife was a mousy woman six years older than he was who had two young children. Their marriage worked until problems cropped up when he attempted to discipline the kids. She chastised him; her kids were her business, not his. But, in fact, the children got no discipline from anyone, and because they were terrors, they became the central focus of the marriage. Doug finally decided he had to get out even though he hated the idea of another divorce. He thought he would never remarry; he was done.

Then he met Vanessa at a class he took at night. She was a young redhead, beautiful, and fiery-tempered. They had a highly charged relationship. After a few months, he asked her to move in with him. He thought this was a way to have the benefits of marriage without the risks. Ah, but that is a foolish idea, as he would find out. The couple lived together about a year, and then she moved out. He said they just couldn't get along. When she got upset, which was all the time, she threw china or anything else she could find. A month after they broke up, she moved back in because Doug believed he couldn't live without her. They kept repeating the pattern of moving in and out. The third time they got back together, she told him their problem was his lack of commitment. Doug decided he had to make this work; he couldn't take another breakup. He had tried to live without her, and every time they parted, he came crawling back. So why try to break it off permanently? He reasoned that his best hope was to get married and stay married. The marriage lasted less than three months. They broke up right on schedule, just like they did when they were simply living together. Nothing was different except for the legal mess they had to untangle. But at least that put an end to the bleeding—it was their final breakup.

The problem was that Doug approached any new relationship with abject fear of having another failed marriage. By asking Vanessa to move in, he was treating the relationship like a test market and ignoring the moral issue. No risk, he thought. If it doesn't work, she will just move out. No pain, no problem. Living together, however, has many of the same problems as marriage. Certainly you face the pain of possible breakup…unless you treat the other person like a boarder. Obviously Doug didn't, and he got very tangled up with Vanessa, especially in the sexual arena. Their on-again off-again romance tied him in knots. When Vanessa blamed the problem on his lack of commitment, that idea seemed plausible so he bit. Neither party came out whole. A divorce after three months is painful, and you have the legal, emotional, and moral problems that go with it. Both should have known better. They had plenty of evidence that showed them this relationship wasn't working.

Erika Wants John, Who Wants Out

Erika, a pretty, somewhat heavy woman in her forties joined our divorce recovery group for one reason—to find a way to hold on to her boyfriend, John. She'd been married once before, and now she had a second chance with John. But he had not only moved out, he moved to the other side of the country. She told us that John was a handsome fellow about age 35 who never seemed to settle down with anyone. Nevertheless, Erika was hoping to learn some tricks for luring John back. Her story about him made our hair stand on end. This guy was a louse, no doubt about it. He'd already been married twice before and had pulled the same thing with his prior wives. He promised all kinds of things, got each woman to marry him, and left after she gave birth to a child. He loved the fun of being with a wife, but he couldn't handle the responsibility of children. Erika even found out that he had done the same thing with another woman whom he had never married. John had abandoned children all over the country.

Now you may wonder why Erika wanted to have anything to do with such a bad-news guy. I wanted to know, too, because it was totally illogical. Others in the recovery group tried to talk her out of having further contact with him, but nothing worked—she spoke with him every week. It didn't even matter that he was already living with another woman. He kept telling Erika he might come back. He claimed he still loved her, missed her, yada, yada, yada. Erika behaved like a complete fool, the way outsiders saw it. The guy was just stringing her along in case his new girlfriend didn't work out. So why didn't Erika break it off?

Erika finally admitted that she'd dated another guy recently, and at the end of their evening, she asked him, "Well, are you interested?" He told her things might work out if she would lose 50 pounds. That cruel comment sent Erika reeling. She concluded that her only chance for a relationship was John. If she couldn't get him back, her future was set. She could only be a single woman alone. In spite of all the evidence about John, she didn't want to break up. She wanted to marry him. No one could fathom why she just didn't get it. When a partner shows he's a loser, why order a serving of that?

Erika had a very false vision of marriage. That's why she allowed herself to hold on to a bad relationship and even wanted to turn it into a marriage. She held the belief that marriage can make someone stay with you or change his bad behaviors. John's consistent loving-and-leaving should have been enough to make any sane person run for the door. But Erika had low self-esteem, which made her think this guy was her only chance for having a man.

A Live Fish Can Bite You

When you have a "fish on the line," you may find it hard to play catch and release. You don't want the breaking-up fallout of pain, dislocation, and the trouble of starting a new future. In addition, since you can't predict what the future holds, you can become very insecure about it and create a scenario in your mind that tells you no one else is going to want you, or that you can't do any better than the person you are with. So why not try to make this one work? Why not accept your gloomy fate and settle for what you have?

If your relationship is crumbling, marriage won't fix it. That's like the old myth that having a baby will glue together a bad marriage. Don't believe it. If time has shown that your relationship isn't rewarding or that it's actually fairly miserable, let it go. Euthanize it. Pay the price upfront and move on. That live fish on the line can bite you if you don't let it go.

Are You at Risk?

Having someone in your life can be enough to make you agree to marriage. But remember that many people who knew better than to marry wound up regretting their decision to go forward. Are you at risk for giving in to the proposition of marriage just because you have a ready and willing partner? Do you...

- think you should break up with the person you're dating but you lack the nerve?
- see that your partner just can't commit even though you've been together for years?
- believe that if you don't marry the one you're dating, you will never get another chance to marry?

- assume that you can't do any better than the one you're dating so you may as well get married?
- fear that you'll be very upset if you "fire" your partner, and he moves and finds someone else?
- assume that you're obligated to marry your current partner despite your serious reservations?
- figure you should marry because it's easier than having to break up with your partner?
- believe that marriage will solve your relationship problems?

If you answer yes to even one of these, you're moving toward a mistake-motivated marriage. Here are some tips to help you avoid another marriage mess-up.

Size up the negatives. Make a list of the positives and negatives about your partner. Assume (realistically) that the negatives won't change after the wedding and that these qualities could get worse. Remember, you get your partner's best face and "party manners" when you're dating. Ask yourself this tough question: Can I live with these particular drawbacks and problems if we marry? If the answer is no, get out before you do something you will regret.

Work on building your self-confidence. If you're staying in a bad relationship, you probably have some self-esteem issues. Fantasize about things that would change your mind about yourself. For example, would you feel more confident if you had a new career or job, a new wardrobe, a makeover, new friends, more money, more people wanting to date you? Now that you've figured that out, develop a plan to make these things that would boost your confidence happen. This may take time, but it's a lot easier than settling for another bad marriage and potential divorce.

Learn to live alone. Another reason you may stick with an unsatisfactory, dead-end relationship is fear of living alone. Why not try something radical like moving into your own place? Or get a roommate (not a lover roommate). If you can't afford your own place right now, follow the tips in chapter 8, "Somebody's Going to Move in Here."

"I was in the service and tired of living on the ship; plus, I was just tired of living alone. I met a nice young lady in a club and had a very good time dancing with her, so I popped the question and she accepted. I really didn't know how to back out of the deal even though we did wait for about a year. I felt that since I had given my word, I should go through with the marriage. The marriage did last for eight years, but there were some bad times that we really shouldn't have put ourselves through because she wasn't really ready to be married either." C.G.

"I wanted security and thought no one else would love me so I'd better marry this guy. He thought I was really good to him, which I was. He asked me to marry him to try to make me happy. To get me to marry him, he made promises that never came true. I was lonely and scared as a single mother and wanted a dad for my son." S.W.

"When I told him that we would have to get married or break up, I didn't think he would say yes. Then I didn't know how to break it off.... We got divorced, but we are still friends." H.L.

"My second husband and I were living together. He wanted to get married, but I didn't. He said that we should either get married or split up. I didn't want to split up, so I married him. It wasn't smart." Y.F.

"We had lived together for several years, and it was time to get married or break up." L.S.

14
Wrong Reason #10
Found My Soul Mate

❧ ❧ ❧

A great marriage is not when
the "perfect couple" come together.
It is when an imperfect couple learns
to enjoy their differences.

DAVE MEURER

The purpose of this book is to help you find the right one to marry. Unfortunately, some people use very strange criteria in making that decision. They have some limited set of characteristics in their heads that tell them when they've found Mr. or Ms. Right. How often have you heard someone say, "I'm getting married because I found my soul mate"?

He Knows My Inner Being

Never fully defined in any literature, the term "soul mate" is used by people as if we all clearly understood what is meant. We have asked a number of people to explain what a soul mate is. We never get the same answer. Nevertheless, it's a popular buzzword. Some definitions of a soul mate is a person who...

- has the same background as you.
- thinks like you.
- understands you.
- knows you before even really knowing you.
- knows you better than you know yourself.
- you can talk with for hours even when you first meet.
- has the same interests and hobbies as you.
- has your best interests at heart.

Others say a soul mate…

- sees into your inner being.
- is like the missing half of you.
- is a perfect match for you.
- is your twin or counterpart.
- is the one, true person for you.
- immediately connects with you.

If you think there is *only one* person out there who is the right one for you, you are vulnerable to marry when you *think* you have found that person. There is much evidence that there are likely many people in the world who would make an acceptable mate for you. The risk of thinking otherwise is that when you believe you have found "*the one,*" you abandon all sensibility and are driven to marry that person. Some people believe in soul mates because of their divorce experience. It didn't work with my ex because he was the "wrong one." Now I will go and find the right one, who will be the opposite of my ex.

Since you believe there is such a thing as the one soul mate in the world for you, you have some preconceived notions in mind. Some people are searching for someone "just like me." Others believe that someone is their soul mate if they have similar backgrounds, thoughts, or views. Still others believe they will intuitively know a soul mate by their connectedness to them. We're not saying that having things in common isn't important. Quite the contrary, it is very relevant in a successful marriage. The problem comes when you are on a mission to find an individual who has one or a few narrow set of similarities or characteristics, and you take it as a sign to marry.

Finding a soul mate is a great *start*, but people are multidimensional. You cannot judge a person as right for you because he or she has certain similarities or just seems tuned in to you. Now you need to spend considerable time learning all about other aspects, such as the differences between you, the habits and quirks he has, any shared values, dreams, goals, opinions, and so forth. Don't fall into the trap of the "soul mate mentality" and think someone is right just based on initial impressions.

When He Said Soul Mate, I Knew...

Sheila was married for 17 years to an advertising executive who was never at home. Their marriage happened because she got pregnant during their dating phase, and they got married to legitimize their offspring. Sheila had three children by the age of 36. The lack of availability of her husband drove Sheila to have an affair with the husband of a friend. This relationship went on undetected for four years before Sheila finally decided she could not handle the strain any longer. At that point she asked for a divorce. Once divorced, the friend's husband quickly backed out of their tryst. She was suddenly available and a threat to his current marriage.

Sheila did not date for more than a year. Then she began to go out with some men from the office. She expanded this to men friends recommended. This intensive dating went on for more than three years. At first, Sheila didn't want to remarry, and she gave off that vibe. However, as time passed, she became more and more frustrated. She decided she needed to find her soul mate. When asked what such a man would be like, she answered by saying, "He will know me better than I know myself." We heard nothing more from her until a friend said she met a man and got engaged.

Later, Sheila said Phil was the man she had been searching for. She knew he was "the one" when he opened the car door for her. He wasn't like the others she had dated. She and Phil immediately hit it off when he told her he was looking for his soul mate. That triggered a discussion for hours. They were of one accord. Sheila did marry Phil, almost immediately. Problems began early because Phil was about to be laid off at work, something he failed to mention during courtship. This put an immediate strain on the marriage. Phil had to sell his home, and they had to move into a small apartment. The pressures eventually forced Sheila to realize that Phil was not her "soul mate," and she filed for divorce.

Sheila let herself become a victim of the "soul mate mentality." After intensively dating men with her attitude of "I'm not interested," she suddenly got desperate and devised a simple formula for deciding when to get married. They would both be of one accord—meaning he would be looking for a soul mate, too. Phil fit the bill, and his gentlemanly courtship behavior was icing on the cake. No need to dig any further in learning more about him or determining if they were compatible in various areas. Being in tune with each other was enough.

We're Just Alike

Andy and Joyce had led a hard life until they met. Andy married a girl in high school, divorced before 19, and dropped out of college at 20. He had one job after another. He never could earn enough money to even afford to take someone out on a date. He moved back home to live with his mother. This made things worse because his self-esteem dropped even further. His older sister and brother were both successful professionals, which was salt in his wound. From early childhood, Andy's mother acted as if she thought Andy was a loser. He'd had poor grades in high school, a failed marriage, a failed college career, and a failing business career all before the age of 25. The more he failed at something, the more his mother reinforced that he was a loser. He acted out her script of a person who could do nothing right. It was a vicious cycle of negative feedback and failure.

Andy met Joyce when a mutual friend suggested they would have a lot in common. Sure enough, the friend was correct. Joyce had grown up in the same town, yet she and Andy had never met. When they began comparing notes, they found tremendous similarities. Joyce's mother was a very controlling woman who judged Joyce and always found her lacking. No matter what Joyce did or accomplished, it was never good enough for her mother. As a result, Joyce had developed an overeating problem in her teen years. Whenever she tried to lose weight, some conflict would develop with her mother and cause a setback. Even when Joyce went away to college, her "failure in her head" mentality kept her from achieving what she knew she was capable of. Joyce had even tried marriage. In her sophomore year, she married a graduate student who left her after seven months. She attributed the marriage debacle to her eating disorder. She always blamed herself for whatever went wrong.

Andy and Joyce saw in each other some amazing similarities that they interpreted as signs that they were meant for each other. Their relationship seemed to help them, too, because instead of dragging each other down, they were mutually supportive. For the first time, they began to feel good about themselves. There were some red flags, however. Occasionally, if Joyce became depressed, Andy couldn't handle it. They even separated one time because of this. Another problem was that Joyce was Catholic and Andy was Jewish. Joyce's mother was totally opposed to the couple marrying. Also, Joyce wanted children, and Andy wasn't sure. He'd had so much trouble as a child, he didn't know if he could be a good father.

In spite of these issues, the couple believed that their similarities were the signal that they were right for each other. Joyce was happy to act in opposition to the wishes of her domineering mother. Andy and Joyce's marriage lasted 11 years, but most of the final 6 were stress-filled. Joyce had again retreated to her illness of overeating, which caused tension in the marriage. Andy continued his struggle to hold a job for more than a year at a time. His out-of-work periods created great financial strain on the marriage. They were not the only ones to suffer from the marriage failure. They had a child who was constantly caught in the middle of the downward spiral of his parents. Some years after the divorce, Joyce committed suicide.

Andy and Joyce were a sad couple who identified with each other's circumstances and mindsets. Two halves don't make a whole, but they thought so. Andy was not ready to care for and support another wife. Joyce was still struggling with her overeating disease and was far from mentally healthy. They ignored all the red flags that were obvious to both of them. No doubt, they each believed no one else would have them, and so this was their one opportunity to remarry. When you find someone who has some similarities to you, it is not enough of a basis for a healthy marriage. Andy and Joyce confused similar backgrounds, conditions, and problems with shared interests, dreams, and goals. They had none of those.

His Children Caused Our Divorce

Belinda married a man when she was in her twenties, and it didn't work out. He told her she was smarter than he was; she made him feel inferior. Belinda was smart, talented, and beautiful. For some men, that's a threat.

By her mid-thirties, Belinda married again. This time she picked an older man, Frank, who was a senior executive at the company where she worked. He had also been married before and had three sons—two who were teenagers and the third of college age. Belinda had no children, and she had originally worried how well she might be accepted by Frank's children. As it turned out, they seemed to love her and she blended in well with his family. All went fine until the couple began to squabble. In these instances, Frank would drag his sons into the fight, and they took sides with him. It got so bad that Belinda demanded that the three boys not be allowed in their home. The friction was aggravating an already deteriorating situation. This angered Frank and brought everything to a head. Eventually Frank and Belinda divorced. She told all her friends that she would never again marry a man with children. In fact, she felt so strongly about this that she would not even consider dating someone who was divorced with kids.

Mark had recently moved to town and joined the church where Belinda attended. Mark had never been married and was a little younger than Belinda. When she met him, she set her sights on him as the next "Mr. Belinda." Nothing would get in her way. He was the perfect candidate. Never married, no children, and no baggage—she thought. They were married, and Belinda found out differently after the wedding. She had never asked if he had children and only found out when she accidentally opened an envelope from one of his past live-ins asking for child support money. Mark had (intentionally) failed to mention that he had lived with two women and had fathered a child with one. He had been too ashamed to tell her this during their short courtship.

Belinda "learned" from her first marriage that a man who has children is not a good husband. She, therefore, concluded that if she could find a man who has no children, she should seriously consider marrying him. This so-called "learning" came about from not allowing enough time to understand what really went wrong in her first marriage and, instead, blaming the presence of her husband's children for the breakup.

The One-Dimensional Match

What do these stories have in common? They may seem very different, but they are all examples of having one dimension in mind as a trigger for concluding, "I have found the right one. I am ready to remarry." Sheila was searching for the illusive soul mate. This thinking focused her on a limited dimension of a prospective spouse—someone whom she would immediately "recognize" as her soul mate. This kept her from examining all aspects of her relationship with Phil. How could she be aware of any negative factors with him after concluding from the start "he's the one"? When you jump to a conclusion that fast, you are assuming all other aspects are irrelevant or will magically work out.

Andy and Joyce identified one important aspect in their lives that they had in common—others thought they were losers. They had become convinced themselves, and so immediately decided to huddle together against the world. Anyone who is feeling so incomplete and inadequate should not consider marriage in that condition. If you already feel like a failure, there is nothing worse than to jump into another marriage, get another divorce, and "prove" it to yourself all over again. You don't have to have the intense mental problems Joyce had. The normal emotional stress of a divorce can place you in the same condition. This story is not a case of rescue. It's a case of believing you should marry someone because he or she is in the same predicament you are. Misery loves company.

When you divorce, you immediately look for the culprit. With a lot of time passed, you will see things differently. You will learn what you contributed to your marriage failing. Time helps us see more clearly when the anger and grieving are past. If you don't wait for that time to elapse before doing a post-mortem on the marriage, you are likely to conclude something very narrow like Belinda did: The divorce occurred because her husband had children. Armed with this "fact," she set out to find a childless husband replacement.

The Perfect Person

We have heard many other versions of this story—where a divorced individual has a "perfect" person in mind. The ideal usually relates to one attribute—often the reverse of what the ex-spouse had. He doesn't drink. She won't be such a religious fanatic. He won't travel in his job. She won't have an ex-husband who lives in town. From these examples, you can write the story about what happened in the previous marriage. Is it wrong to be concerned about issues such as these, especially if they were a problem in your past marriage? No, of course not. The problem is one-dimensional searching: When you are so focused on one issue you tend to ignore other things. Because someone you date has or doesn't have the characteristic you are looking for is no guarantee of success in marriage. You still have to do the hard work and allow the time to make sure he or she has other good qualities and not any horrible ones. You also have to be observant of the dynamics between you. How do you two interact in various circumstances? What does he do that causes conflict? How does she behave when under pressure? To gauge all of this takes time, an open mind, and an objective attitude. It sounds cold and calculating, but remember, divorce is painful and affects your entire family.

Sign of an Unhealed Divorce

Another reason that single-dimension searching is a problem is that it is a sign of an unhealed divorce. Think about it. Sheila sought a soul mate believing that was what was missing in her prior marriage. She was frantically dating. She was frustrated and desperate. Does this sound like a woman who has allowed time to pass and worked through her problems to become healthy and independent?

Then we have Andy and Joyce, two people who needed to get their own acts together before putting their problems on each other. They were each still struggling with low self-esteem from childhood, which was reinforced in their previous divorces. Andy was still living at home with mom. Joyce was unable to control overeating, a clue that she was not well.

Finally, Belinda had gone through two marriages and was still confused about what had happened. When you are still blaming someone else for the failure of your marriage, you need to remain in recovery and accept what you did and learn forgiveness. Belinda wasn't close to accomplishing that. She was still playing the blame game.

If you are on a one-track search for Mr. or Ms. Right, you are not ready to remarry. Don't get confused when you date that because someone has what you deem desirable similarities to you, this is enough of a basis for marrying.

Are You at Risk?

Searching for a soul mate can be dangerous. Are you at risk for this behavior? Do you...

- have a "soul mate mentality"?
- believe you will know the "right one" the minute you meet him or her?

- search for your next spouse looking for one important trait—maybe the opposite of what your ex had?

- think there is only one person in the world who is right for you, and you are on a mission to find him or her?

- have a set of criteria for the ideal spouse or a simple formula for knowing who would be your soul mate?

Here are some tips to help you avoid trapping yourself in the soul mate myth.

Retrain your thinking. If you have a "soul mate mentality," educate yourself about the risks. One way to do this is to read and reread the stories in this book of redivorced people who naively searched for their soul mates only to get burned because they refused to see or acknowledge any problems once they made up their minds.

Don't shop for duplicates or opposites. Finding your mirror-image mate in background or experience is no assurance of a good match. Likewise, just because someone doesn't have the ugly habits or traits of your ex (drinking, yelling, spending, controlling) doesn't mean he will be right for you, either. List the problems of your past marriage(s) and make certain that these are not the only criteria you use to select a future spouse.

Don't be unequally yoked. If you choose someone who has a major difference in belief systems from you, it is likely to become a problem after the "honeymoon phase" is over. When your most fundamental beliefs are at odds, you will eventually see divisions creep into the marriage that could lead to its downfall. Any disagreements or major differences in belief systems will certainly become more pronounced if and when children are part of your family.

Allow enough time dating. Quick decisions about a soul mate can be overcome if you date someone at least a few years before marrying. Be alert to problems and red flags.

"I really thought she was my soul mate, but in hindsight realize that I didn't really know her. I had been divorced for four years and had been dating a lot but not meeting anyone who I felt wasn't materialistic. I met her on an airplane, and we carried on a long-distance relationship before getting married a year later. Unbeknownst to me, she was on the rebound from a relationship with a man who had gotten another woman pregnant and had moved in with her. She told me that she loved children (I had two) and wanted to have children. That was baloney." S.M.

"We were so in love we had to be together. We thought we were soul mates. We lived together two years before we married. We were married thirteen years. We thought we would be together forever but things changed. We raised my three children and his two children. We retired, and he was home all the time. My mother wasn't well enough to live alone so we moved her in with us. Everything changed again, and my 'soul mate' became mentally and physically abusive." E.M.

"My wife had died less than a year before I met this one, and I guess I missed the married life and companionship. When we first met and for several months it seemed like we both liked the same things, basically home, motorcycles, fishing, and other things. I thought she was a true soul mate. But she was quite a bit younger than I. That didn't seem to matter at first. After about 6 months of marriage I noticed some tension between us. Just little things at first, but of course they grew until it was apparent to both of us that our real goals in life were very different." T.J.

~ ❧ ~

"We liked doing things together, had similar interests, and convinced ourselves that we were in love. I was starting a new job that required me to be away from home for extended periods of time. She wanted an available husband. We gradually grew apart. It only lasted 5 months." K.E.

~ ❧ ~

"Thought I found a soul mate. We were really different personality types, had different goals & dreams. We felt our differences would enhance our feelings for each other. We were wrong." N.B.

~ ❧ ~

"After meeting and having a brief and passionate time together, I thought that we were soul mates. As it turns out, she was not honest about her feelings and later said that she never loved me." V.U.

15
Wrong Reason #11
Money: That's What I Want

❧ ❧ ❧

They say love and marriage
go hand in hand. But add money
to that equation and entire relationships can,
and almost always do, entirely change.

SUSIE GHARIB
Nightly Business Report

Money drives a lot of people to do a lot of things they shouldn't. Remarriage happens to be one of them.

Divorce Divides

Can two people divide what they have and be as well off as they were before? Not likely. Even in community property states, which mandate an equal division of assets, dividing two into anything is less than what you had before. Even people who are well-to-do often have their lifestyles altered by divorce. After a split you need two residences, two cars, two sets of dishes, two of everything. Even the tax laws work against divorced people.

Do people remarry for money? There is a lot of evidence that they do. Some of the people in the survey confided that money, or the lack of it, drove them to the altar. Others said they knew that the person they mistakenly remarried was interested in them only because of their money. Look how many trophy wives (and trophy husbands) you see nowadays. Statistical evidence shows that women, in particular, are less well off after divorce. Studies reveal that directly after divorce, men are a little worse off, but eventually become better off. In contrast, women are significantly worse off. They usually have the responsibility of raising the children. Many have not worked for some time, and their skills are not up to date. Women, on average, earn less than men. Put all the pieces together, and it's not surprising that many women believe their financial problems could be quickly solved by remarriage. Is it wrong to remarry with the hope of improving your financial situation? No. The problem occurs when money motivates you to remarry, and you overlook other factors critical to a successful marriage. Even if no subsequent divorce occurs, you can be awfully unhappy if you remarry just for money. Sooner or later you are going to have to look at your partner and decide if you like him in the cold light of day when he is not writing checks. Suddenly an exit from the prison of your indebtedness to this spouse might sound tempting.

Reasons People Remarry for Money

Rescue. How does money motivate remarriage mistakes? We already discussed the rescue issue, when someone is in dire straits and needs to find a spouse with dough. The opposite side of that coin is the divorced person seeking a spouse who uses his or her money to lure in a prospect.

Money was a problem. If your previous marriage had money problems at the top of the list as reasons for the divorce, you are likely to seek out someone who has enough so it won't be a problem in the next marriage. In this case, you have enough money, so it's not a rescue situation. Instead, you're focused on finding Mr. or Ms. Right who, by definition, also has the bucks so that money won't be an issue in the marriage.

Regaining a lifestyle. Another draw for a moneyed spouse is when you had plenty of money in your previous marriage. In fact, you and your ex led a very high lifestyle. Now, after divorce, you have to scale back considerably. If you could find a new spouse who also has a large bank account, you could resume the life you had and are sure you deserve.

You were cheated. If in your previous marriage you felt cheated because there was never enough money to do what you wanted, you might decide not to make that mistake again. In this case, money may not have been a problem in the marriage. You just saw wealthy friends buy this and that while you had to settle for less than luxury items. As one ex-wife told me, "You can marry more money in 15 minutes than you can make in a lifetime."

You could be taken. If after your divorce you ended up with a large nest egg, you may worry that someone will come along and woo you to get a piece of that pile. This is quite common for women who are left with a substantial sum at separation. You don't want to be "taken to the cleaners." But if he has plenty of his own money, then you have more confidence he is not marrying you for money, and he will not attempt to drain you.

There are plenty of other reasons people remarry for money. We are just not creative enough to think of all of them. But we have heard plenty of stories, so we know it happens often. There is nothing wrong with being conscious of the financial situation of a remarriage prospect. Having been married and learned how important money and financial management is in marriage, you would be a fool to ignore the topic. Who wants to get into a marriage situation where your new spouse cannot even support himself or has a gambling problem or is a spendaholic? Being careful to select a mate who is responsible with money is crucial to the success of the next marriage. Having money be such a dominant force in your calculations that you remarry because of it is a different story.

She Talked About Nothing but Money

Butch was a budding successful attorney by the age of 37. When he married Carol, who was 28, she had nothing. She worked for a legal courier firm. Over the next 8 years, they created a luxury lifestyle for themselves. They had a beautiful, five-bedroom home, three luxury cars, a boat, and closets full of clothes. They lacked nothing. They didn't save any money, either. The couple had two children, ages three and five.

On his forty-fifth birthday, Butch began to act strangely. He started coming home late from work. He avoided Carol and the children. He wouldn't talk about what was happening. In divorce recovery, Carol told us that Butch kept saying life was passing him by. He felt trapped. He had to do something to change the situation. So he told Carol he was leaving and that they should separate for a time until he could gain his footing. The couple did separate. Butch moved into a rented, furnished house. For a time, they both tried to continue as if nothing had changed. But the debt began piling up, and there were unpaid bills every month. The pressure became too great, and they mutually agreed to file for divorce.

Carol had to sell the house. The children were now put on a strict budget, and frequently she had to tell them no to purchases. Butch paid some alimony and child support, but his payments were sporadic. Carol faced a new, diminished lifestyle. Still, she wore a diamond-encrusted Rolex watch and drove a Mercedes. She talked about nothing but money and money problems. Carol was a very bitter woman. She acted as if life owed her the lifestyle she had with Butch, and she had been cheated out of it. She said she could not face some of her previous friends because they still had the means to do whatever they wanted. It made her envious and, at the same time, embarrassed. Carol looked with disdain at other people in the divorce recovery group who were clearly of a lesser economic status than she used to be. You might even say she was a snob. It was puzzling. She grew up in a modest family, had nothing when she met Butch, and now acted superior to everyone around her. We attributed it to the shame, insecurity, and disappointment of her totally unexpected divorce. Carol was not in the kind of emotional and financial circumstances where she should make a remarriage decision. That was our advice. She ignored it.

During our divorce recovery sessions, Carol began talking about a man she met—Shawn. He was her cousin's friend that she met at a family party. Shawn had been married and divorced three times before. He owned a large building supply company in town. He was very wealthy. He wined and dined all the women he dated, and Carol was no exception. We heard the rest of the story later from Shawn.

He said Carol came after him in a big way. She told him on the first date, "You are going to marry me!" Shawn was lonely and discouraged about marriage after his earlier, unsuccessful attempts, and he was tired of dating. He was vulnerable. This was a fatal attraction. Before marrying, he suggested that he and Carol visit a psychologist friend who was a marriage and family counselor. Shawn feared another failed marriage. After three sessions, the psychologist advised him against it. He told Shawn that Carol had not yet recovered from her divorce and was preoccupied with money. Since Shawn had a lot of money, this last part didn't faze him.

Shawn went through with marrying Carol some months later. He told us later that he knew better. He said during their brief dating time, an episode happened that set him back. When he corrected Carol's youngest son about something he was doing, Carol went into a tirade. She normally had a mild demeanor, but when she got angry, she was a wild woman. This situation almost ended the relationship, even though a marriage date had already been set. We asked Shawn, "Then why did you go through with it?" "Loneliness and sex," he said. Once they were married, everything broke loose. Carol started demanding money for all kinds of things. She became hostile when Shawn attempted to reason with her about her behavior. The issues with her children proved to be a problem as well because they resented Shawn, and Carol always took their side. The marriage ended in a year and a half.

The remarriage of Shawn and Carol ended in divorce because neither party was ready to remarry. Carol was so devastated financially from her first marriage that she was driven to find a man who could restore her upscale lifestyle. Instead of readjusting to reality or deciding to develop a career of her own that could provide substantial income, she focused on finding a "sugar daddy." Poor Shawn was the intended victim. It's hard to feel sorry for Shawn, though, because he saw a glimpse of Carol's personality, her reaction to his involvement with her children, and had a psychologist's recommendation, and yet chose to ignore all of it. His big spending habits while dating also sent a signal: If you marry me, you will have lots of money. This type of advertising attracts gold diggers.

As discussed previously, when lovemaking is a major factor in choosing to remarry, you set yourself up for inevitable disappointment. No marriage remains as hot as it is during the early phase. Marriage is about finding a compatible roommate as much as it is a lover. If you're fighting or upset with someone, it's difficult to be in the mood to be loving. In addition to the obvious issues mentioned, Carol should have at least been skeptical because Shawn already had three marriages that terminated. Allowing time to understand who Shawn was, what might have happened in those marriages, and what he had learned from them to avoid a repeat would have minimized her chance of being ex number four.

Bucks on the Brain

If money is always on your mind, you have a problem. Either you are living above your means or you want to. Experts agree that money problems are often a major cause of divorce. And divorce creates money problems initially for almost everyone. Usually some of the ugliest fights during divorce are about money. Given this, isn't it logical that in divorce recovery you should work on ways to solve your own money problems? When you look for others who will do it for you through marriage, the risks are great. You will pay one way or the other.

Another hard lesson here is to be willing to back out of a situation when evidence piles up suggesting you should not go through with the marriage. We cannot tell you how many times we have heard divorced people say they knew there were problems before the marriage, and they went ahead anyway. Some went so far as to admit they knew the odds were greater than 50 percent that the remarriage would fail, and they still got remarried! If you are emotionally or financially vulnerable, and you let yourself get too involved with the other person, it's hard to think straight and pull the plug. Don't date seriously until you have recovered from your divorce. Wait until your vulnerability level goes way down. Also, be open to what others tell you about what they see. They are not always correct, but if a close friend or counselor tells you not to marry someone, take it as a serious red flag that deserves your attention and consideration. At a minimum, give the situation more time before marrying so that you have an increased chance of learning more about your intended mate.

Are You at Risk?

In the national survey, almost as many people mentioned money as love. Money can put you in a position where you will do things you would not ordinarily consider, like choosing the wrong person to marry. Are you at risk for this situation? Do you...

- have serious financial problems?
- see no way out of your debt crisis?
- feel tremendous stress because of creditors?
- lack money even for necessities?
- feel angry or cheated because you have had to significantly lower your standard of living after divorce?
- wish a wealthy suitor would come to your rescue?
- find yourself dating someone who needs you to pay his bills?
- find yourself dating someone just because he or she has money?
- fear someone is going to drain your dough?

Here are some tips for dealing with money issues without resorting to remarrying.

Put money in perspective. If you don't have money to pay your grocery bills, that's one thing. But if you are not really poor, realize that you probably have much more than many other people. Life is not all about money. You have your family, friends, and even material things that few in the world have. People driven to recover losses from a divorce may pay a heavy price. Focusing on money can steal your joy and contentment.

Get financial advice. Many people have no aptitude for managing their finances. If this describes you, get advice. If you can afford a financial planner, go for it. If not, there are many sources such as accountants, stockbrokers, bank personnel, and even knowledgeable friends or spouses of friends who will help you if you ask. You can also check out "Credit and Debt Counseling" in the yellow pages of your phone book. Many nonprofits don't charge for an initial consultation on your situation.

Develop a plan to live within your means. In the short run, you may need to balance income and expenses so that you don't rack up debt or go through any assets you retained from the former marriage. We have seen couples divorce and have to sell their homes. Then they proceed to live off the equity. That works in the short run, but how will you be able to afford another home? While you are draining the equity, home prices are probably rising. Soon you may not have even enough for a down payment. Since a home is the most valuable asset you are likely to have, you want to be able to own one again eventually.

Develop a long-term plan to accomplish your goals. Make a list of your goals, such as getting more education, buying a new car, sending your children to college. Now you will need a long-term plan for how you will accomplish these. It may require you to retrain for a new career, change your lifestyle, or even reevaluate your goals.

"I was looking for romance, love, and a true soul mate. My ex-spouse was looking for nothing more than someone to take care of her monetarily. She was not in it for true love. Once the money was gone, so was she. The old saying 'love is blind' held true in my case. I did not see all the signs that other people saw but did not say or tell me about until afterward." W. J.

~ ✻ ~

"My wrong reason: We got married because it seemed like the fiscally sensible thing to do. We felt that if we merged our assets we would be in a better position to develop a more fiscally 'sound' position with which we could improve upon on a timely basis. It did not work at all. She was too greedy and wanted everything for herself." L.E.

~ ✻ ~

"He just wanted a meal ticket. I had a good job, a new car, and was fairly attractive. He said all the things I needed to hear." T.F.

~ ✻ ~

"I thought I was in love, but after the marriage he quit his job and wanted to just spend all my savings. It cost me $20,000 to get out of the marriage. I thought that I was 'in love.' We married too fast in less than 6 months. We both were consultants working in another state. We were together 24 hrs a day & thought that we had passed the test, so to speak. What I didn't realize then was that since we only knew each other through work and we were living thousands of miles from home, we didn't see each other in the context of our home situations. Essentially, he was able to recreate himself in a way. I only knew what he presented himself to be. He was an amateur actor, and he was good.

He played the part of the man I wanted, not who he was. In retrospect, I think that my ex saw that I had an income at least as high as his, and he needed help paying off a mountain of debt. He was a serial marry-er—I was #4. Once the dew was off the rose (about 5 years), he moved on to #5—our next door neighbor. Not coincidentally, most of his personal debt had been paid off or converted into joint debt by then." H.T.

~ *❀* ~

"He was wealthy. I pressured him into marriage because of a strong need for security on my part." L.U.

~ *❀* ~

"I think he married for the companionship, and I married to get out of a financial situation and to not be single any more. We met through a personal's ad and hit it off from the beginning. Even though he was a lot quieter than me, I thought that it was something I could live with. Turns out he was something of a recluse and couldn't handle strangers coming into our home. We did have a similar interest of getting outdoors and motorcycle riding and walking together, but the conversation just stopped after that, and it wasn't enough to stimulate me. I also married him because he was a kind person and very giving. We enjoyed sharing quiet times together." Y.D.

~ *❀* ~

"My ex-husband and I dated for two months. Before I met him, he was told I was wealthy, which I'm not. He was in financial trouble—so, basically, everything he said to me (about himself, etc.) was false. He lied from the beginning about himself. He also didn't tell me about a multitude of things, such as a repossessed car, loans he had and was not paying, etc. I ended up asking him to leave after only 8 or 9 months, when my accounts started being garnished to pay for his debts." P.P.

~ ✲ ~

"I had four children and their father resisted paying child support, so when I met this man I needed help with the mortgage and food and other necessities of life. I could only get work as a substitute teacher at the time, and that is irregular work that does not pay very well. So when he proposed, I jumped at the chance. All he wanted was someone to cook and wash, so I really exchanged housekeeping services for maintenance for my children, who, by the way, hated him." C.M.

~ ✲ ~

"My ex-spouse wanted to marry me for financial reasons. He wanted to start a business. He had no money and had bad credit. On the other hand, I had an excellent job, savings, property, and an excellent credit rating. I thought it was love. He started the business (which was successful), and he also started fooling around within a year of the marriage." V.J.

~ ✲ ~

"I was virtually unable to provide for my own living and found an older lady who found my company tolerable. I had a place to live but would have been unable to pay the rent after my roommate moved out to pursue a relationship. This lady wanted to be with me more every day and felt it more acceptable to marry than 'shack-up.' I am Catholic and found marriage to be undesirable because it would not be in keeping with the church. But marriage seemed like the only way out of the insecurity of not being able to economically survive by myself. I was not madly in love, and I feel she was as needy for the security of companionship as I was for security of sharing expenses with someone 'more permanent than a roommate.' It was not an unpleasant relationship even up to the divorce from my standpoint." T.A.

16
Wrong Reason #12
For the Children's Sake

❧ ❧ ❧

Whenever I date a guy, I think,
"Is this the man I want
my children to spend their weekends with?"

RITA RUDNER

Divorce is devastating for children. Some are caught in the middle during the parental fighting prior to the divorce. Others are told out-of-the-blue the shocking news that daddy and mommy don't love each other anymore and daddy or mommy is leaving. Children fear they will be abandoned. They think the leaving parent doesn't love them. They may even think they caused the breakup. If you have children from your prior marriage, you know all the problems divorce creates for children and for single parents.

Some spouses believe they can never be an adequate single parent. Then there are the likely fights, sometimes in a courtroom, over visitation and support issues. The responsibility of being a single parent is frightening and a great challenge. At the same time you are grieving or battling with your ex, you have to remain calm and rational with your kids. If you are the parent the children will live with, you have one set of problems. If you are the parent who doesn't have physical custody of your children, you have another set. You can divorce your spouse, but you should not divorce your kids. If you are the one who left home and want an ongoing relationship with them, you have to have some type of cordial relationship with your ex to accomplish this. That's not always easy.

Sometimes kids are put in the middle of the divorce when each adult lets the children know what daddy or mommy did wrong. "We had to leave your father because he spent all of our money." "Mommy left because she loves someone else." Sometimes people use the children as messengers to the ex: "You tell mommy that I won't give her that ring." Sometimes they are asked to be spies: "Who is daddy dating?"

I Need a Father/Mother Replacement

The pressures of single parenthood drive many people to remarry to fix the problems the divorce caused for the children and for them.

Children need a father/mother. You may believe your children will grow up disadvantaged unless they have both a father and mother at home. You have read the statistics that reveal that children who grow up with both parents at home have more financial and educational advantages than youngsters raised by one parent.

I cannot make it alone as a parent. You may be overwhelmed by the challenges and feel the stress of single parenthood. You have to be a disciplinarian, a teacher, a financial provider, a homemaker, a chauffeur, and a role model for your children. If the pressures get too great, you have a strong desire to "get help" from a new spouse.

Set an example. Maybe you have someone in your life, but you don't want to live with him. This would set a bad example for your kids. Or you want to have intimacy with someone you're dating, but you don't feel right about bringing him or her into your home with the children present. Getting married would solve this problem.

Humpty Dumpty. You and your children are likely traumatized by the breakup of your family. Your goal is to put everyone back together in any way possible. One way is to get a substitute father or mother through remarriage. The belief is that life will go back to like it was before because there is a mother and father present again.

Let's Make a Deal

"I had to do it for the children." That's what Yolanda told us was the reason she got remarried. Yolanda was a happily married housewife of 33 with two young girls when her husband told her he was involved with another woman. Their breakup left Yolanda and the children in terrible circumstances. In the divorce, the husband gave Yolanda the house, and the court mandated payments for alimony and child support. But the money amount was insufficient to maintain the home and cover the needs of her girls. The real problem for Yolanda was that she had been a very dependent wife who counted on her husband to do everything. Without him, she was frightened about all the responsibilities she had.

Yolanda knew she had to go to work, but she couldn't afford a maid or babysitter. Even though one child was in school, someone had to pick her up. The younger girl could go to preschool, but that costs money, too. Yolanda's car was five years old, and the high mileage resulted in frequent repairs. But the financial problems were minor compared to what she faced at home.

Right after the divorce, her older daughter would cry all night. Then the teacher told Yolanda that her daughter was hitting other kids in her class. Sometimes she would just have fits in the classroom. The father would call sporadically, which made things even worse. The children would expect him to pick them up or call when he said he would, but then he wouldn't show up or call. He always had excuses. Yolanda got some free counseling from school personnel and from her priest, but the problems continued no matter what she did. Both children frequently said they believed their father didn't love them, and they were afraid their mother would leave them, too.

In divorce recovery, Yolanda was so preoccupied with her parenting problems that she could not devote any attention to her own feelings about her divorce. She told us she had joined the local chapter of Parents Without Partners (PWP) in hopes of learning more about how to be a successful single parent.

Russell was 42 and a widower with three children of his own. Two were teenage boys and the other a preteen girl. He and Yolanda met in PWP and soon realized they might help each other. At first it was just picking kids up from school, going out to eat together, and going to movies. Within two months after their arrangement began, Russell suggested they should consider marriage in order to make a better life for their children. His children needed a mother. He was not a great cook and had difficulty being patient with the problems teenagers have. Yolanda said she was thrilled at the prospect of having a full-time man around the house. She added that the extra income wouldn't hurt, either. When we asked her if she was in love with Russell, she said that was "high school stuff." Love didn't make her first marriage last. Now she felt a more mature attitude was to first look at the practical benefits to the children. She could learn to love Russell over time.

Days after the wedding, when they moved in together, Yolanda knew she had made a mistake. Blended families are hard work, and Russell wasn't up to it. Once married, he wanted to dump his children off on Yolanda. He didn't do anything around the house. And he paid little attention to Yolanda's girls. The teenagers were already rebellious, and they became extra ornery when Yolanda tried to act like their mother. In as much time as it took Yolanda and her husband to decide to marry, they decided to "unmarry."

Experts say new stepparents should not to try to be instant fathers or mothers to the children of the new spouse. In a blended family, the true parent has to continue to take responsibility for his or her children. (For more on this, check out Jim Smoke's *Seven Keys to a Healthy Blended Family*.) Russell was hoping that Yolanda would simply unburden him from that necessity. Yolanda approached the marital relationship to Russell as a business deal.

There are complications in a remarriage because of children, exes, grandparents, and so on that do require a practical orientation. You can't just drive off into the sunset like you could when you were young and have no responsibilities. Yolanda's belief that being in love was not important, maybe that it was even childish, ignored the fact that being in love with someone is what gets couples through the rough spots. Without love, the relationship broke down immediately when Russell didn't hold up his part of the implied contract.

The Moral of the Story

Government statistics reveal there is a greater chance of divorce in a remarriage when there are children present from either party vs. when neither party has children at home. Knowing this, people have to be careful before remarriage. Getting to know the other person's children and developing a plan for how to handle the inevitable conflicts that will come should be mandatory before saying "I do."

Remarriage to solve the problem of the "missing parent" is not a good idea. Living with someone else's children can be extremely difficult. Making blended families function well is hard work. If you think marrying to get a substitute father or mother will make life easier, you will be in for a shock. If you have learned to handle the needs and problems of your own family, you may benefit from remarrying. But if you think remarrying will lighten the load and be a panacea for family bliss, this is the wrong reason to remarry, and you're likely to regret it.

Are You at Risk?

Whether being well meaning or by guilt, people do remarry for their children's sake. This is an honorable objective to consider, along with all the other factors we discuss in this book. Here are some clues to help you evaluate whether you are at risk. Do you...

- feel you desperately need help raising your children?
- believe your kids would be better off if they had the missing mom or dad?
- feel guilty because you can't give your children everything you would like?

- feel guilty because you left your ex and broke up the family?

- think you are inadequate as both a mother and a father?

- think you would settle for someone less than what you might normally demand to benefit the children?

Rather than remarrying to provide the "missing" parent, try some of these.

Learn the facts. With so many children now being raised in one-parent households, there are tremendous resources available to you. Check the Internet to see a list of them. Parents Without Partners is available in most medium to large cities. New evidence reveals that children are better off in a one-parent home if there was hostility previously. Also, many kids raised by a single parent do perform as well in school and in life as those in two-parent households. In contrast, children in a home with a stepparent do not necessarily do better.

Deal with your guilt another way. If the guilt of breaking up the home is troubling you, deal with it in a more constructive way than remarrying. List the reasons you left your spouse or he left you and the impact it was having on the family. This will help you keep in focus the reason a divorce was justified.

Take parenting classes. Most areas have classes available to help you become a better parent. A supplemental benefit is that you will meet others in your situation who can provide a support group. You may find people who can trade chores with you. For example, they could babysit your children, and you can help them with cooking or yard work.

"I was a single mom raising three kids alone. I was having financial problems and had moved in with my mother. I met this man through a friend, and we hit it off extremely well. He liked my kids and went out of his way to be thoughtful and include them in things we did. I was thrilled to find someone who cared so much about my kids and was willing to share in their upbringing. After dating about four months, he asked me to marry him. He said he was tired of waking up alone. Turned out it was a case of 'Dr. Jekyll & Mr. Hyde.' We were married just over a year. I finally had enough of his verbal and physical abuse and told him to get out." L.Q.

"I was on my way to another divorce! I was devastated but couldn't live under the circumstances: a cheating husband who insisted he loved me and wanted to correct the wrong and stay married. I was lying across my bed crying when my 15-year-old (mature beyond his years) came in and asked why I was so upset when I had made the decision to get another divorce. I told him I had let him and his brother down; I'd failed again! He told me that I had to quit looking for a daddy for him and his brother. That I was more mother and father by myself then most of his friends had with two parents! I have not been married since, and the love I receive from all of my children is more than any one person could ask for." T.L.

"My first husband (of 18 years) got into his car one afternoon and drove off out of state leaving me, three beautiful children, a business, and our home. After two years, exhausted and broke, I finally agreed to marry the man who had been asking me to marry him since my first husband left. I married him thinking it would help the children and improve our situation. It didn't, and so I divorced again." G.W.

~ ❧ ~

"I was widowed with two children and thought I needed help raising my children." A.T.

~ ❧ ~

"I felt that the remarrying was for the wrong reason because of my children. I wanted the children to see that it is wrong to live together with a man, that you should be married. This was a big mistake. I should have gone back to living alone when my children came back home from living with my ex. Once we were married things changed. Also my children were unhappy to see me with a man other than their father. If I could have turned the clock back I would have never gotten married until my children were out on their own. You do things at times not knowing how it is going to turn out, and this marriage was a big mistake. You try to give values to your children, and one of the values I wanted them to know was not to just live with a man or woman, that you should be married first." C.P.

~ ❧ ~

"The man I dated talked me into getting married, was romantic, etc. Also, he said my kids need a 'father figure' in their lives for stability, etc. As the kids got older, he treated my sons very badly…he was verbally and emotionally abusive. It got to the point that when they turned 18, he was going to put them out on the street. He made our lives miserable. He was a mean, bitter person. I knew he meant what he said about putting the boys out, so I left him before my oldest son turned 18. P.S. He died seven years later. There is justice!" B.N.

~ ❧ ~

"Thought I needed help raising my two sons. Did not date much and, as I was getting older, I figured I would not be able to find anyone to marry." S.K.

"The person that I married was a total opposite of my first husband....He represented stability and financial security, which was absent in my first marriage. He seemed like a nice person, had a daughter, and I had no children. I liked the idea of a family. He wanted stability, didn't want to be alone, and wanted help parenting his daughter...she was eight when I met him, and I don't think he knew what to do with her. He had terrible parenting skills. We married after only ten months. There were some red flags...but I ignored them." T.J.

"My ex and I were together for approximately seven years. He had two children that he was completely involved with and had them most of the time. I wanted the relationship to work and did a lot of things to 'mother' the children and create a positive, happy home environment. My ex really wanted someone to be their 'mother' and take on all responsibilities while he worked and continued his hobbies, etc. He didn't want to discipline, handle school issues, etc. After the oldest daughter moved in with us, I took on the role more diligently as 'mother,' and he didn't like how things were being handled. He decided in less than a year he didn't want to be married (I was his third); however, less than a year after the divorce, he remarried." F.G.

"I had custody of my children from a previous marriage. I thought being married again would provide a positive role model for my children (all girls). I liked being married. I wanted to wait and have a longer engagement, but I gave in to her and got married sooner. I found out after we were married that she had money, emotional, and mental problems. A longer engagement would have revealed those things before getting married. My fault for not insisting on a longer engagement." H.H.

17
Wrong Reason #13
It's a Couples' World

❧ ❧ ❧

Marriage is like a cage; one sees the birds
outside desperate to get in, and those inside
equally desperate to get out.

MICHEL DE MONTAIGNE

Being single again after being married is not easy. It seems particularly difficult for those who have been married many years and then get divorced. Women seem to have a particularly rough time in the adjustment. If you get divorced at age 25 or even 35, you probably have not been married for a significant amount of time, so it has not been that long since you were single. Also, as census data reveals (see chapter 22), there are still many unmarried people who are available in these younger-age categories. But if you are 45 or older, you may have been married for 10 to 20 years. If you are 55, maybe it has been 30-plus years since you were single. The adjustments get tougher the longer you were married and the further away you are from having operated as a single person.

Left Out

What are the adjustments divorced people talk about? The number one thing we hear is best summed up by the expression: "It's a couples' world." Some use words suggesting they are left out or excluded. Here is a short list of some of the adjustments and problems newly divorced people relay in their comments:

- My married friends don't call me as often.
- My best friend now acts like I am a threat to her marriage since I am "available."
- The single people I have met so far are not quality people.
- The good ones are taken.
- It's difficult to go to a restaurant or movie by myself because I feel self-conscious.
- Most of the events at church are for couples.
- I couldn't stand going to singles-type bars. They are meat markets.
- When I go to a party, I'm odd man out since every one of my friends is married.
- I am apprehensive about asking a man to go out. He may get the wrong idea.
- Women today are very aggressive; not like when I was single 30 years ago.
- It seems like most women are looking for a rich husband.
- I tried going to a few singles events, but they are so boring.
- When I tell people I am single (at my age), they immediately look askance at me.
- I hate shopping and cooking for one.
- It's hard to do the things I used to do like sports and go to plays by myself.

- I am always afraid to have a repair person come to my house.

Being married for many years and then being yanked kicking and screaming into the single world is a traumatic change. It's not about loneliness per se. Many of the people who complain about these adjustments are not really saying they are upset because they are lonely. They have friends. They have families. They have activities. The discomfort is the pressure of being an outsider or an alien from most others they know because they are now single. Establishing a satisfactory social life and adjusting to these new circumstances is critical to recovering from divorce. Unfortunately, some people want to take what they think is the easy way out—quickly getting remarried.

Not All Men Are as Wonderful as Larry

Sharon was married to Larry at the age of 22. They met in college and became immediate best friends. When they graduated, they got married. Within six years, they had two children. Their marriage was, according to all their friends, a model marriage. When I met the couple, they had been married for 31 years. They got up every morning and went to Starbucks together at 7:00 AM. They frequently met for lunch. Larry was an insurance agent, and he took Sharon to all the conventions. She always helped him arrange meetings with clients and helped schedule his day. They were inseparable. Totally unexpectedly, at age 54, Larry had a massive heart attack and dropped dead on their living room floor. Sharon was devastated and completely lost. All her friends said she would never get over Larry, and she would never remarry because they were so intertwined.

But her friends were wrong. Sharon grieved and spent time recovering for more than two years. Then she seemed to snap out of her focus on the past and became focused on replacing Larry. Sharon hated being single. She always felt left out. She was happy being married, and she wanted to be married again. A friend told her that every marriage isn't as ideal as the one she had, and that she had to be careful and not assume that all men are as wonderful as Larry. Because Sharon had never been divorced and didn't have the feelings of rejection that can accompany divorce, she was more idealistic about marriage than maybe she should have been. It's great to be positive and optimistic; it's another to be naive and unwise. Sharon was acting like the latter. When she dated a man, she would immediately bring up the idea of marriage. She frightened away a number of prospects. One man dated her for three months but finally told her she was moving too fast for him. It was just a question of time before she hooked a vulnerable soul.

Burt was the unlucky one. He had been divorced for a year and a half, but he hated every minute of it. He attributed the divorce to a laundry list of his wife's problems. At the top of the list, he said she was too pushy and wanted to run his life. When Burt came into the picture, Sharon suggested they begin to do many of the things she had done with Larry. Suddenly she was a couple again. Married friends invited them over. They even joined a couple's connection group at her church. Sharon's social life changed dramatically again—for the better. Burt, on the other hand, did not respond so positively to the changes. He was basically a very introverted guy who just liked to stay home and watch basketball and football. Sharon had no interest in either. While Sharon had a strong Christian background, Burt, who had Christian parents, had little interest in religion.

Finally, Sharon told Burt that it was time they got married. People were beginning to talk. Whatever apprehensions he had about going through with it, he put aside because he didn't want to stay single. They were married—and lived to regret it. Once married, Burt turned out to be nothing like Larry—surprise! This couple is still unhappily together, but only because neither of them wants to be single again.

Sharon was not ready to remarry, but she wanted to be a couple again. She couldn't see any reality about Burt except that marrying him would accomplish her goal. Sharon should have seen the problems that would beset the marriage since she did get to know Burt well enough to know his personality, interests, and habits. Those she did see that were problematic, she ignored. This wasn't a case of love is blind. It was a case of getting married to avoid staying single at all costs.

Burt had not had sufficient time to recover from his divorce. The very fact that he still focused on what his wife did wrong rather than his role in the marriage dissolution was a sign that he was far from ready to remarry. There was every reason to assume that whatever problems Burt had, he was doomed to repeat them in the next marriage because he had obviously learned nothing from the experience. The loneliness factor for Burt made him susceptible to any woman who would fill in for his ex-wife.

The Benefits of Singledom

Sharon and Burt didn't allow enough time to recover and become independent from their losses. Even in the case of the death of a spouse, many of the same issues are relevant for recovery. Sharon was still needy in her unquenching desire to remarry to get back into the world she knew—married couples. How can you avoid this problem if you are disturbed about being single again? You have to acknowledge your new status and make the decisions that you will develop a new life for yourself, become happy as a single person, and take advantage of all the benefits that singledom offers. You can do this by making a list of the things that you can now do that you couldn't do before and the things you can still do that you did. You will find that there are really very few things that you can no longer do as a single person. Accept that your ex is gone, and recognize the exciting potential of getting to know new people and do new things. When you date without expectation, the pressure is dramatically reduced.

Is it always greener on the other side? Many unhappily married people wish they could be single again, to be without the responsibilities and being tied down to someone they no longer love. Many unhappily divorced people believe their lives will begin again when the wedding bells ring. Widowed people are particularly vulnerable to this myth because if they were happy in their marriages before their spouses' deaths, they automatically believe being single is a sub-par existence and happiness is just a wedding ring away.

Only 55 percent of men and 52 percent of women are married today in the U.S. Note that is barely over half. All the rest have never married or are divorced, widowed, or separated. But there aren't that many unhappy people in the country. It's only "a couples' world" for half the population, so let go of that myth.

Are You at Risk?

If you fear you are at risk for marrying to avoid being single, test yourself with these questions. Do you...

- believe it's a couples' world?
- hate being single?
- have no or few single friends and don't want to have any?
- feel that marriage is the only "normal" state?
- feel excluded from social events and activities because you are not married?
- think of yourself as an outsider with your married friends?

Try some of these to get you out of this dilemma.

Get a (single) life. Acknowledge you are single, and quit fighting it. If you are divorced, you know you can be miserable being married. Don't assume marrying anyone will make you happy again. Find a new set of friends—single and divorced—if you feel too removed from your old married ones.

Deal with your loneliness. "Couples' world" thinking may be another way of saying you're lonely. If that's the underlying problem, use some of the suggestions in chapter 8, "Somebody's Going to Move in Here."

Ask your married friends to include you. A widow we know asked her friends to occasionally include her when they go out to dinner.

Sometimes married couples simply don't think to do that. Also, they may assume you would not be interested or you are too busy. Ask.

Pursue new activities you might not have tried when you were married. Being single does have the advantage that you don't have to always consider another person's feelings in what you choose to do. Now you can try some of the things that your ex refused to do.

"I was tired of not being a part of what was considered normal. I felt like life was passing me by. I had a small child that I was raising by myself. I had moved away from where I had lots of friends, and I was lonely. He pursued me vigorously and said things like 'whatever it takes…' My son was almost always included on our dates. When I started to see his temper, I had already arranged some of the details of the wedding and told my parents. But I went ahead anyway." J.O.

"I had been single for about five years and didn't like single life. My girlfriend thought I was the kind of person she could get along with. She liked nightclubs and country clubs and knew that I didn't like them. I still can't understand how we decided to get married." M.K.

"I didn't like being single, when everyone I knew was married. I thought it would be my only chance to marry again. He seemed perfect at first, and we liked all the same things…I thought. I think I wanted to show everyone that I was attractive to someone." B.J.

"I was a single mother of a three year old….My friends were all couples, and I was tired of being alone. Wanted married life again. Hitched in five months. Thought I knew him, but was wrong…found out for sure when he was drunk in public, threatening me, and had to be subdued by the police." N.E.

18

Marrying for the Right Reasons

❧ ❧ ❧

Two people were talking. One said:
"I got married because I was tired of eating out,
cleaning the house, doing the laundry,
and wearing shabby clothes."
"Amazing," said the second. "I just got divorced
for the very same reasons."

Before addressing the right reasons to remarry, let's revisit the wrong reasons and see what percentage of our national survey participants made these mistakes in remarriage. The 500 redivorced people read a statement describing each of the 13 wrong reasons and answered whether he/she believed that was a reason for his/her redivorce. Recall that 88 percent agreed that they remarried for one or more of these wrong reasons.

Remarrying for Wrong Reasons: Survey Results

Rescue Me. Remarrying to save yourself from your problems, often ones that are the result of your divorce. Also, you could be remarrying to save someone else from his problems in the mistaken

belief that he or she will then need you and not leave you like your ex did. (The key problems here are insecurity and neediness.)
Surveyed people agreed: Men 15%; Women 15%.

I'll Show You. Remarrying to get revenge or prove something to yourself or your ex because you feel rejected.
Surveyed people agreed: Men 7%; Women 6%.

Stop the Dating Game. Remarrying out of frustration because dating is hard, and you're unwilling to do it. Or you remarry because you have dated so many without finding the right one, so you settle.
Surveyed people agreed: Men 12%; Women 5%.

Somebody's Going to Move in Here. Remarrying out of loneliness. Suddenly finding yourself alone is one of the biggest issues for divorced people. The desire to end loneliness can motivate an unwise remarriage because you fail to look for or you overlook relevant issues or problems with your fiancé.
Surveyed people agreed: Men 39%; Women 28%.

Romance Me, I'm Yours. Remarrying for romance or sex. This can happen when you're in love with love or addicted to it. You become vulnerable to people who chase you or romance you. You overlook red flags. Remarrying because of romantic actions or sex can be a fatal attraction.
Surveyed people agreed: Men 33%; Women 44%.

Jump-start My Life. Remarrying someone because you are bored and have the mistaken belief that a mate will make you happy or complete your unfulfilled life.
Surveyed people agreed: Men 5%; Women 3%.

Feeling the Pressure. Remarrying because of pressure from family,

friends, coworkers, religious advisors, counselors, or the person you are dating, when you actually know better or have reservations.
Surveyed people agreed: Men 4%; Women 5%.

It's Time. Remarrying because you believe it is time to do so. This can be a result of your biological clock ticking, the feeling that you've dated long enough, or the feeling of being left out since everyone else you know is married.
Surveyed people agreed: Men 23%; Women 11%.

A Fish on the Line. Remarrying because you have a live prospect or you feel an obligation to marry because the only other option is a painful breakup.
Surveyed people agreed: Men 15%; Women 12%.

Found My Soul Mate. Remarrying with closed eyes and a closed mind. This can happen if you have a "soul mate mentality" because you're looking for a person who fits a preconceived notion of your ideal. You think, "I'll know him/her the minute we meet." This type of thinking results in unpleasant surprises.
Surveyed people agreed: Men 32%; Women 22%.

Money: That's What I Want. Remarrying when you have financial problems that you expect your marriage partner to solve. Also, trading up, recapturing your diminished lifestyle, or protecting yourself from gold diggers.
Surveyed people agreed: Men 8%; Women 11%.

For the Children's Sake. Remarrying to give your children the missing parent or to help you cope with the responsibility thrust upon you from divorce. You seek a quick father/mother replacement out of guilt or belief that the children will be better off.
Surveyed people agreed: Men 7%; Women 12%.

It's a Couples' World. Remarrying to avoid being in the world of singles. This can especially happen if you hate being suddenly single after years of marriage—your social world is turned upside down. Remarriage puts you back in the couples' world.

Surveyed people agreed: Men 11%; Women 8%.

Summarizing the results of the survey, we see that men are most likely to make a remarriage mistake due to loneliness and women from clouded thinking when they're being romanced. Many of the other wrong reasons also plagued the survey people as shown in the table below.

Summary of Wrong Reasons to Remarry Given by Participants in the National Survey			
Men		**Women**	
Somebody's Going to Move in Here	39%	Romance Me, I'm Yours	44%
Romance Me, I'm Yours	33%	Somebody's Going to Move in Here	28%
Found My Soul Mate	32%	Found My Soul Mate	22%
It's Time	23%	Rescue Me	15%
Rescue Me	15%	For the Children's Sake	12%
A Fish on the Line	15%	A Fish on the Line	12%
Stop the Dating Game	12%	Money: That's What I Want	11%
It's a Couples' World	11%	It's Time	11%
Money: That's What I Want	8%	It's a Couples' World	8%
I'll Show You	7%	I'll Show You	6%
For the Children's Sake	7%	Stop the Dating Game	5%
Jump-start My Life	5%	Feeling the Pressure	5%
Feeling the Pressure	4%	Jump-start My Life	3%

What Do These Wrong Reasons Have in Common?

One-dimensional focus: Many of these wrong reasons to remarry are one-dimensional. You are focused on one thing in your search for a mate, and that's someone who will provide money, someone who will be there so you won't be lonely, someone to ease you out of the chore of dating, someone who brings you flowers, someone who will make you laugh, someone who will be a co-parent and so forth. There is much more to the decision to remarry and to pick a suitable mate than just solving a one-dimensional problem. Almost anyone could fill the bill for some of these simple needs. However, people do go that route, and that's why their marriages fail. You'll marry anyone who can take care of that one thing, and you may overlook his or her negatives. But that person isn't likely to meet all your other needs.

Selfish motivation. Another thing the wrong reasons have in common is they are self-serving. They are all selfish. You're looking to get something, not to give something. The wrong reasons are all responses to "I need." Anytime you marry for selfish reasons alone, you implicitly put the other person under pressure to deliver something that he or she may be unable or unwilling to give throughout the marriage. We all know when we're being used, and that's definitely not the basis for a happy marriage.

Desperate behavior. Most of the situations described in this book's anecdotes are from people who were desperate at the time they remarried, which is quite understandable in one sense. When you get a divorce, you are in emotional upheaval. You can't think straight. You flail about, thinking "maybe I can make it" and then "no way I can make it" and everything in-between. Should you make a critical life decision in this condition? No. Is remarriage a critical decision? Yes. One thing is for sure—after divorce you need time to heal and grow whole again.

Red Flags

Wrong reasons to remarry are really cases of wrong place/time/ situation. You remarry when you're not ready because you find yourself in difficult circumstances and somehow decide that another person can fix your problems. Often these circumstances are caused by the previous divorce.

Marrying to solve problems you should have solved yourself. When divorce occurs, you face tremendous strains, and some of the problems you inherit are tough to manage. You need to devote time and effort to solving these problems and becoming proficient in your new responsibilities. Initially, you are lonely, and you face some rough quandaries:

- You haven't become financially independent.
- You may not know how to be a good single parent yet.
- You haven't developed a social life as a single person.
- You haven't dated enough people to know exactly what type of person suits you best.
- You haven't figured out what role you played in your failed marriage and learned from it so that you won't repeat the same mistakes in your next marriage.
- You still need to work on learning about yourself.
- You still need to solve your own problems.

Be your own best critic. If you see you're looking for someone to solve problems that you yourself need to fix, catch yourself and recognize the red flag.

Marrying too quickly. When people remarry for selfish wrong reasons, they generally marry too quickly. You may not want to wait for years to get your problems resolved. You're ready to have someone pay your bills right now. You're ready to stop dating. You need someone to help you with your unruly children. Whatever problem you're having, you want a person who can step up to the plate ASAP. But can you really get to know someone in three or six months…or even a year? Do you know what your new mate will be like under the pressures and problems of living? Typically, finding out those things takes time.

Surveyed people who said they remarried too quickly: Men 33%; Women 37%. Look at what some of these surveyed people said.

> "After a 21-year marriage and then a divorce, I remarried too quickly. I missed the family setting, so that was why I remarried. I didn't take the time to think clearly and think things through." H.D.

"I had been divorced 3 years after being married for 27 years. I guess I felt that no one would ever be interested in me at my age and that I was lucky to find someone who wanted to be with me. We married after only dating for a few months, and I didn't really know who he was. I realized after a few months that I had made a big mistake but decided to make the best of it. He asked for a divorce when we had been married less than a year. I found out later that he had been seeing someone for quite some time. I guess that I shouldn't have been surprised, especially when he told me that he maintained an affair while his first wife was dying of cancer." F.B.

"I had only been divorced six months, and my second husband was different from the one I had just divorced. I rushed into a second marriage without really knowing what I wanted for my life and not finding out what he wanted. I thought that if we were enjoying each other's company, that was love and it would last." C.M.

Marrying someone you hardly knew. Sometimes people marry before they get to know their partners well enough. Remember, your prospective spouse probably got a divorce, too. What was the reason? Does he or she have traits you should know about before you walk down the aisle? Desperate people don't usually scrutinize the baggage of prospective partners carefully enough.

Surveyed people who said they remarried someone they hardly knew: Men 16%; Women 27%.

"I didn't really know her well enough to see what was coming. I thought being married would make life easier." V.K.

"I didn't realize it then, but I just didn't know the type of person he was. We came from totally different backgrounds, with different beliefs and morals. And love is blind." S.J.

"My second divorce happened because I didn't know the guy very well. My first divorce had a lot to do with in-laws interfering in our relationship, and we were very young. I didn't take the time to get to know him, and I really should have. If I had, maybe I would have put two and two together and figured out that he cheated around on the three other wives before me." P.P.

Marrying someone you knew better than to marry. If you hope to solve personal problems via another person, you can overlook a lot of things if that person can meet your needs in the area where you are deficient. You may even admit that you knew your fiancé had big problems, but you overlooked them and went ahead. You desperately want someone to fill that hole in you or solve your problems that keep you from acting in a rational manner. Look how many times you read about people who admit that the reasons their marriages failed were there in the open long before the wedding took place. You may have such a story from your last marriage. We just hope we can change the person or learn to live with the tragic flaw.

Survey people said they remarried when they knew better: Men 17%; Women 16%.

"My ex-husband and I were very different people. But I was 'in love' and just overlooked these differences. I thought that love would conquer all." D.A.

"I married the second time because I thought I liked being married. I thought the person I was marrying was a good provider and companion. I knew he was an alcoholic—I did ask before we married, but he assured me he could quit drinking anytime." J.L.

"He was a good man and good to me, but insecurities

caused him to lapse into depression. I married him knowing this because I didn't know how to back out. His family was very close-knit, unlike my own. They treated me like family. I felt very secure with his family. I thought I could change him, but I was very wrong about that, and that just made things worse." M.N.

"I ignored warning indications because it was so late into the commitment, and I thought it could work out, which was the wrong conclusion. Our value systems were too different, and basically, she was a liar in almost everything—very deceptive, devious, and hateful. But I found out too late." T.O.

Marrying because you believed marriage would fix the problems. You may admit you know there are problems with the person you plan to marry or with the relationship, but you plunge in anyway. You hope that marrying will solve the problems.

Surveyed people who agreed: Men 14%; Women 7%.

"I thought that maybe by marrying things would improve in the relationship since he said he loved and needed me to help him to make his life better, as I was the best thing that had happened to him." S.Q.

"We never got along too well when we were together. However, we were miserable being apart. I thought getting married was the solution. Of course, it wasn't. Things got worse when we realized that the problem was that we just couldn't get along. Being married forced us to be together, which made the situation even worse." T.N.

"I had been living with him for a year. I had three teenage children. Things were very stressful, and he was very unhappy. He repeatedly said that the problems were because he wasn't really part of the family. I finally agreed that perhaps getting married would help him feel that he belonged, but I didn't really think through how I felt. I should have backed out of the wedding because a part of me knew it wouldn't work. I couldn't admit that I had made a mistake, even to myself!" B.F.

The Right Reasons to Remarry

Here is what you have been waiting for! You are now going to discover the *right* reasons to remarry. That's why you bought this book.

#1: *You Are in Love*

As mentioned earlier, love is not a sufficient reason by itself to get married, but it is a very important one. Every marriage has its ups and downs over the years. Without love, it's hard to get through the tough spots. Being in love is not the same as the deep-seated love that occurs after many years together. People from countries where arranged marriages are common say that they develop a love for each other even though there was no potential for "falling in love" during courtship. So it is possible to grow to love someone whom you don't have strong feelings for upfront. But why risk that you might not develop such a love if you have little feelings or even somewhat negative ones for him or her at the start? Many redivorced people in the survey said, "I wasn't really in love, but I thought the marriage might work because…"

#2: *You Want to Get Married but Don't Need To*

When you are sufficiently healed from your divorce (or the death of your spouse), you will be able to make clear judgments. Marriage is a contractual bargain and a partnership. You wouldn't do it unless you thought you would be better off and happier than you were being single. You legitimately expect to fulfill your partner's needs. And, in return, you will get love, affection, caring, companionship, money, children, coparenting, social benefits, counsel, sex, and so on…not necessarily in that order.

Yes, these are many of the things we've listed as wrong reasons. What's the difference? Attitude and motivation. When you are in "want" mode instead of "need" mode, you will feel no pressure to marry quickly or to overlook issues. You won't go forward if red flags appear. You will even back out if you conclude your intended is just not the right one—even though it will be painful. When you're happy the way you are, you will be able to choose wisely.

#3: *You Are Able to Give More Than You Get*

Marriages are more likely to succeed when each party is ready to give more than he or she gets. That's one signal that you are ready to remarry. You are ready to take care of another person in a nonrescuing capacity. You are now strong enough that you have something to give. When you are in the throes of divorce or afflicted with Post-Divorce Syndrome, you are totally needy and have little or nothing to give. Marriage is a relationship of sharing, of give and take. There is a natural division of labor that goes something like this: You work, and I'll raise children. You wash the dishes, and I'll cook. You take care of the house, and I'll do the laundry. You take care of me, and I'll take care of you. When the balance of benefits gained and delivered is out of whack, the marriage can falter. If you enter a marriage in a needy state, you're not going to be good at creating an equilibrium of give and take. If you enter a marriage with anger, bitterness, and remorse from your prior marriage, you aren't going to be good company. And if you have serious personal problems, you immediately put a burden on your new spouse. If you want, want, want, the other person will soon know it and resent it. If you are emotionally healthy and approach marriage ready to give (as well as get), the marriage has a much better chance of success. The same goes for your fiancé. If you choose to marry a person who is still in turmoil, you will get turmoil.

Analyze Your Motives: Remarriage Deal-Breakers

When you wonder what are the good reasons to remarry, you really need to be asking what are *your* reasons for wanting to remarry.

Because you love Sam or Samantha is important but not a strong enough reason to get remarried. Here are some recommendations for remarriage stoppers:

- If you feel like you *need* to remarry, don't do it.
- If you have serious, unsolved problems in your life, work on them. Don't try to solve them through a new spouse.
- If you have doubts about someone you want to remarry, stop, allow more time, or back out.
- If you're not happy with your life, don't get remarried until you are.
- If you're not ready to take care of someone else, then take care of yourself first.

When you have recovered from your divorce and you're so okay on your own that you don't *need* to get remarried, you will then be in a good position to know when you're ready. You'll be able to marry the right person for the right reasons. You may find it hard to trust yourself after divorce. You may be afraid to go with your own judgment. But who knows the following better than you?

- What you need.
- The kind of person you're attracted to.
- The person you can get along with.
- The one you believe is the best person for you.

Our best advice: Trust yourself *but only when you're in a position to do so.* The last part of that rule is critical. You can make remarriage mistakes when you're not yet poised to make the best decisions for yourself because divorce has left you still vulnerable. Get yourself on an even keel first. Then find the right one for you.

19

Get Whole!

⁂ ⁂ ⁂

Man is incomplete until he is married.
Then he is finished.

Whole = 1. Complete
    2. Sound; healthy
    3. Restored; healed: a whole man [or
      woman] again
Recovery = 1. To be restoring (oneself) to a
      normal state
    2. To regain a normal or usual
      condition, such as health

Get whole! That's the prescription for avoiding remarrying for the wrong reasons. Not being whole, caused by Post-Divorce Syndrome, is the underlying condition that leads to ill-advised remarriages.

Some may say that "getting whole" sounds like New Age psychobabble. What does it really mean? Essentially, you are whole again when you are restored, healthy, and complete. *You are not looking for someone else to make you complete.* To get whole, you have to go through a process that takes time and effort. We call that process "divorce recovery." Notice we didn't say time or effort. Naomi, a woman in a divorce recovery group, said she waited two years before remarrying. The problem was that she was just as bitter and consumed with her divorce as the first day it occurred. The opposite happened for Brendon. He told our group that he had spent all of two days crying and lamenting his divorce. Then he was ready to forget it and move on. He didn't allow himself to truly evaluate where he had been, where he was now, and where he was going.

This isn't a book on divorce recovery. (See Recommended Reading for a list of excellent books on that subject, including Jim's classic book *Growing Through Divorce*.) You can find divorce recovery groups offered by churches and other organizations. We both teach in this kind of program and are grateful to see tremendous progress when people are willing to do the necessary work.

Some of the salient issues in getting whole again are important to this book because you need to do certain things to inoculate yourself from making the mistake of remarrying for the wrong reasons.

Set Your Goal on Getting Whole

What are the goals in going for wholeness? What will the changes in you look like? What will you accomplish? What outcome will you achieve?

Stability

After divorce, you experience tremendous upheaval. Your emotional, social, and financial situation may well be chaotic. Everything seems changed. With your entire life topsy-turvy, an important goal in recovery is to stabilize yourself first and begin to build a new foundation in these areas: emotions, social structure, and money.

Responsibility

In the early stages of divorce, leaning on others for support is a good idea. But in recovery, you need to begin the process of reasserting yourself as a functioning, responsible adult. This means building self-confidence and taking charge of your life. Children panic when adults whom they depend on are suddenly unable to cope. So do family and friends. Make it your goal to begin taking charge of normal responsibilities and acting in a rational manner.

Knowledge

To avoid repeating past mistakes, learn from your divorce. Jim calls it *growing through divorce*. "You can go through it or grow through it." Growing through it means getting something positive from a horribly unpleasant experience. Remember: Those who fail to learn from history are doomed to repeat it.

Living in the Moment

Here's the dilemma of divorce: You must learn from the past and, at the same time, forget about it. Divorce is a final act signifying an end to a marital relationship. Your goal is to live in the present and refrain from dwelling on the past, which you cannot change. Healthy people put the past behind them and grow in the present.

Independence

The goal is to move away from the needy state that divorce creates at first, to lower your vulnerability level. We have seen how needy people do foolish things. Like an addict, needy divorced people sometimes look for a fix—only via new spouses. Independent divorced people, on the other hand, have a calm demeanor and aren't driven to remarry to resolve holes in their lives.

Taking Baby Steps to Getting Whole

Your steps in divorce recovery are:

- Get free from the past.
- Get a social support structure.
- Get financially stable.
- Get responsible for your children.
- Get learning from your divorce.
- Get closure.
- Get a future.

Not everyone goes through all these steps in the same amount of time or in the same way, but *all steps are necessary.* We have seen people in our divorce recovery program who were completely stuck. They couldn't advance because they were living in the past. In contrast, others want to skip all the steps. They report that in a short time they have already grieved and gotten over it. Now they want to move on to the next step. This just isn't a realistic amount of time to heal. Still others are so wounded that they trust no one and can't even reach out for the help they need.

Simple solutions aren't available to help you recover from divorce because people respond differently to tragedy. Regardless of what you've been through and where you are, you need to go through *all* the steps for complete recovery.

Get Free from the Past

Here are some things to help you break away from your old marriage, your divorce, and your ex.

Acceptance

The starting point to recovery is acknowledgment and acceptance. Just like an alcoholic, if you're in denial, you can't begin to solve your problems. You need to accept that you are divorced. Maybe you didn't want the divorce, but you're now living out the choice that your ex made. Even if you were the one who left, you didn't want this to happen. The important point is to accept your new identity. You are now divorced. Say that with us: I am divorced.

During the mourning phase, go ahead and lean on family and friends for support. Divorce is rough. You have a right to feel terrible. And be prepared for surprises. During Ed's divorces, some people he expected to come through for him just went cold. Some took sides. Others went AWOL. Some even acted like his divorce threatened their marriages. But there were also some pleasant surprises. People he never expected to be supportive came through for him—big time. You may have the same experience.

In the early stages of divorce, you can expect to feel shock, anger, confusion, tearfulness, and every other crazy emotion. Take some comfort in knowing you're certainly not the only one going through divorce. That knowledge makes a big difference. In divorce recovery groups, the first thing people say is, "I can't believe all these people are getting a divorce, too. I thought I was the only one. Guess I'm not alone after all." Sure, misery does love company, and hearing others tell their divorce stories helps put yours in perspective. No matter how bad your story is, there is always someone with a worse tale to tell. And, finally, if you discover that you just can't seem to pull yourself out of the grief stage, get professional help.

Legal Resolution

You don't get free from the past without dealing with it. Ignoring it won't make it go away. You have to stare it down and slog through it. Another task that's required to get free of the past is the resolution of legal problems. Whether your assets are large or small, whether you're childless or the parent of five, you still have to go through the ugly mess dealing with the courts. You should talk to people who have been recently divorced before you visit with an attorney. An attorney's job is to represent you in your confrontation with your ex, and that can be a problem. Why? Because once you get attorneys involved, you have a confrontational situation. Sometimes the only winners are the lawyers.

A relatively recent trend in California is a divorce minus the dueling attorneys, which works if you and your spouse are fairly amicable on decisions about division of assets. Even if you have children, you can deal with the courts without major battles. Because every state has different laws, you can only protect your rights by seeking an understanding of what your options are. Then get legal advice.

Detachment

Sounds silly, we know, but we have to tell some people to let go of their exes. One woman in divorce recovery was still meeting her ex for sex 20 years after the divorce. Another kept inviting her ex over for dinner under the guise of wanting their kids to see that the family was still intact, which was, of course, a myth. One man continued to "date" his wife for two years after breaking up. A woman told of staying in her ex-husband's apartment when she visited his city, even though he was living with another woman at the time. Divorce can make people do insane things. If you don't let go, you can't move on. It's that simple. We tell these people: Pull the plug. Your marriage is history. Your future is somewhere else.

You also detach by moving away from thinking and acting like a victim. At first, maybe you do feel victimized, and you want to vilify your ex, who did you wrong. The problem with playing the role of the victim is that it keeps you mentally tied to your ex. You're thinking, "He did this and that; he was so mean." How can you get free of your ex-spouse and the past if you dwell on it? And friends and family tire quickly of hearing you whine about your trials and sorrows. Another problem of the victimized state is that it prevents you from looking at the complete picture—your role in the divorce. Yes, she left you, but you had mentally abused her for years. Very few divorces are totally one-sided. When someone tells us, "I thought everything was wonderful and then he left," we are suspicious. It rarely happens that way. Maybe one person refuses to look at the problems or reality, and the divorce wakes him up. But more often than not, problems were evident for some time before one person announced he or she was leaving. If you stay a victim, you fail to give yourself the opportunity to learn what truly happened in the marriage.

Recovery Takes Time

Divorce recovery takes time—at least two years. For some, it takes considerably longer. You can't rush healing after open-heart surgery, and you can't rush healing from broken-heart misery. We have seen people become despondent when they are told about the amount of time required to heal. They think, "What a waste. I'm not getting any younger. I need to get on with it." And some do exactly that, usually to their detriment. Many jump into a remarriage that ends just like the previous one. Why not give yourself the luxury of healing slowly, with the almost surefire benefit that you'll be much happier in the long run?

Building Social Support

Nothing can cause chaos in your social life like divorce. People are there to help at first, but then they get busy and get back to their own lives. After the early phase, when you need to lean on friends the most, you need to begin building a new support structure. This means single friends. People who try to hang on only to their married friends miss out on having a full social life. Whether you want to remarry or not, finding other divorced or single friends gives you options you just don't have with your old crowd. Other divorced people have gone through the divorce wars and can identify with your situation. (Just make sure you don't let anyone drag you down with his or her own troubles.) Unlike your married friends, your new single friends are available to do things and go places.

When you divorce, you're suddenly alone, but you can fill that gap with a range of family, old friends, and new friends. If you don't, the specter of lingering loneliness can spur you to grab someone (sometimes just anyone). If you hear yourself pining for "someone to marry," take it as a wake-up call to get out of the house and meet new people. Divorced people often tell us they don't know how to meet new people who are divorced/single. They have become so comfortable over the years they spent with married friends that they don't know where to start. Try divorce recovery groups. Also ask friends, church personnel, and coworkers if they know of any singles groups you could join. With the Baby Boomers entering their fifties and sixties now, you'll find a lot of divorced people in older age groups. Singles groups are not just about kids anymore. According to the U.S. Census, in 2003 there were 33 million divorced or widowed people—the majority 55 and older. Since the average age of first marriage has increased substantially, you'll find huge numbers of single and divorced people in their thirties and forties, too. Only 52 percent of American households are married couples living together. Being divorced doesn't mean having to be alone. Also try to meet people with interests similar to yours. If you love books, join a book club. Lifelong sailor? Find a sailing club. Get involved in hobbies and activities in which you can meet other people. That way you have something immediately in common.

The final step in establishing a social structure is to begin dating. Do this even if you think you never want to remarry. The best way to date is to begin finding friends of the opposite sex whom you enjoy being with. That's a low-intensity way to spend time with people. No expectations, no pressure. If it turns into something more serious, great. If not, you have found a new friend. Many people now meet other singles on the Internet. Some fear this, but if you check people out carefully, it can be a way to meet quality people without going to bars. Many dating and matchmaking services are legitimate. Ask for recommendations from people who have tried this route. Just make sure to be wise and on guard. For instance, always meet someone new in a public place.

Get Financially Stable

Money is often a root cause of strife in marriages, and this issue can be just as big a problem once you are divorced if you don't get a plan to manage your finances. Divorce itself usually causes a range of financial problems, as you know. That's why it's smart to prepare a budget. Hire an accountant to help you create a balance sheet of assets and liabilities and an income statement. You may discover that you need to return to work to make ends meet. Stabilize your financial life so you can live within your means and save for future needs. Living week to week is risky because you have no safety net for emergencies. If you can afford it, see a financial planner for help in setting up a budget and a financial plan for the future.

Take Responsibility for Your Children

Whether you have physical custody of your children or not, you need to figure out how you will help support them emotionally and financially. More than a quarter of children today live with one parent, and more than half will live in a one-parent household at some point in their lives. What this means is that you're not a single-parenting pioneer. Talk to parents who are in this situation and learn from them.

Incidentally, a recent study debunks the notion that children who grow up in single-parent homes have more problems than those in two-parent homes. Stability and health depends on how both parents behave toward their children. You divorced your spouse, not your children, and it is key for both parents to make it clear that is the case. If you're careful to provide plenty of loving reassurance, your children will overcome their fears and the false beliefs they have that they caused the divorce and you don't love them. One reason children in single-parent homes sometimes aren't standouts academically is that many times the helm of the home is directed by a mother who lacks higher education and who has limited means. In these circumstances, the children have fewer advantages, and this is reflected in their schooling and career choices. But you can make it different for your kids. Some suggestions are:

- Don't let your children run your life or use you and your ex against each other.
- Don't put your children in the middle of battles with your ex.
- Don't belittle your ex to your children and make them think less of their other parent. (Remember, that person remains part of their genetic heritage, and they want to be proud of that.)
- Don't try to be both parents to your children. Let your ex do his or her job.
- Don't make your children parent you in your divorced and weakened state. (And don't use your child as a confidante on adult issues.)
- Set boundaries for your children. (They will be testing you, especially when they sense that you're weak and vulnerable.)
- Have a plan for your children's visitation with your ex and be flexible. You want your children to see their other parent without having to get frustrated by adult games.

- Keep the children's activities going. Avoid disrupting their lives as much as possible.
- Tell your children the truth about financial matters so they know you trust them.

This is just a smattering of the kinds of advice you can get from the many books on how to raise children in a single-parent home. The goal for you is to establish a routine that makes your children stable and comfortable and keeps you from feeling pressured to find a replacement spouse/parent.

Gaining Knowledge from Your Divorce

When people come to our divorce recovery groups fresh from a divorce or in the middle of it, they are in no position to learn anything because they are angry and can see only one thing clearly: Their spouses are nasty creeps who caused the breakup and the hurts they're feeling. At that time, it's useless to ask them what role they played in it. If you're in that scenario, you'll probably just say you were the victim, and you didn't do anything wrong. At the outset, we all play the blame game and don't want to discuss anything else. This gets old to family and friends. So check yourself to see if you're still telling everyone you meet about all the wrongs that have been done to you. It's healthy to vent your anger and frustration, but you don't want to let that evolve into a core of bitterness because then your healing stops cold.

If you're still talking about how evil your ex is, try this exercise. Say to yourself: I know that he or she was mainly at fault in the divorce, but I was also responsible because I _____. At first you will mention trivial things. I didn't take out the garbage. I complained when he wanted to watch football. And so on. But don't stop there. Ask it every day, if necessary:

- What else did I do?
- What did my mate say was the reason he or she left?
- Why did I leave?
- What problems did we have?
- What did we fight about?

- What were the things that kept coming up?
- What were our frustrations?
- What didn't we talk about?

This game of questions can help you begin to acknowledge that you had a role in the disintegration of the marriage. The point isn't placing blame or guilt, but helping you learn what you did so that you don't enter a new marriage and become a repeat offender. You may have to forgive your ex before you can actually look at the breakup objectively. If this doesn't move you toward looking for your part, ask a close friend who spent time with both of you for opinions on why your marriage ended and your role in it. Professional counselors can help, too, if you are stuck.

Dueling Dynamics

When you begin your post-mortem of the marriage, be aware that interpersonal dynamics play a large role in failing marriages. It's not just that your mate had this fatal trait and you had that one. Some marriages don't work simply because of the dynamics of the interactions of the people involved. You could be totally different with a different spouse.

One of the reasons the divorce rate has grown over the years is that these days people aren't willing to stay in an unsatisfactory relationship long-term. Maybe one or both partners aren't willing to do the extremely hard work and make the sacrifices necessary to turn the marriage around.

Having been married a number of times, Ed can report that every marriage was different. "True, I was the common denominator, and they didn't work. I was the same person in every marriage, but the marriages were all different because the dynamics of interaction were different each time. For example, in one of my previous marriages, my wife was very sensitive to criticism because of the relationship she had growing up with her father. I, being a consultant, have the habit of giving advice, which was a real drawback in the marriage. This dynamic proved disastrous and was a constant source of friction. Conversely, my current wife is not sensitive to suggestion, so no such problem exists with her. It's important for me to understand this unfortunate trait I have so that I don't sound controlling or demeaning."

Note what we are saying: You need to look for answers as to what went wrong in your marriage and what your role was in it. When you remarry, the dynamics are likely to be different and so will the responses. Nevertheless, you should seek to understand what you did last time that could be causes of conflict in your next relationship.

Get Closure

How do you really put the past behind you and move forward without it being an albatross? The answer comes in forgiveness—the most critical step in divorce recovery. Forgiveness is the capstone to a recovery program because when you forgive, you're ready for the next phase in your life. Because of that, you should seriously consider the importance of thoroughly forgiving your ex-spouse. Yes, we're talking about the one who hurt you so much. You may be thinking, "Well, dream on because that's never going to happen." But it can happen. We will show you why you should forgive, and we will show you how to do it.

Forgiveness Is the Key to Healing Yourself

Forgiveness, by definition, is pardoning or excusing someone for a fault or offense, or renouncing anger or resentment against that person. When we ask you to forgive your ex, we are not asking you to excuse the wrongs because what your spouse did may be inexcusable. Nevertheless, you need to forgive. *Forgiveness is the key to healing yourself.* You'll see why after you absorb the following stories.

A man said that he could not forgive his ex. Eleven years ago he got a divorce after his wife had an affair. She then promptly moved in with this man, further embarrassing him. For the entire 11 years, he has stayed angry and frequently reviewed how evil and hurtful she was. He said he could not forgive her ever. Why should he? She wronged him.

A young woman related the story of a husband who constantly spent money with credit cards and racked up huge debts. The couple often could not pay bills and were hounded by creditors. Finally the wife demanded a divorce, and after it was final, she wanted nothing more to do with him even though they had a three-year-old daughter. Whenever his name was mentioned, she went into a tirade.

A middle-aged woman said she stayed married to a man who was physically abusive toward her and her children for more than ten years. She endured the pain because she had no way to support the children on her own. The marriage ended when her husband left her for a younger woman. She felt guilty that she allowed her children to be abused by her lack of action and because she never had the courage to end the marriage on her own. She hated her ex-husband and sometimes had thoughts of killing him.

A man had been divorced for five years, and he was still fuming about the coworker who had an affair with his wife. The wife eventually left to be with this coworker. The husband didn't blame his wife. He blamed the coworker who seduced her and promised her things that the husband could not give her.

Who is the primary victim in each example? Who is damaged the most from this lack of forgiveness? And why should a person so wronged, sometimes horribly wronged, even consider forgiving the one who did the injury? Simply put: *You are the victim of your hate, bitterness, resentment, and unforgiveness.* Your feelings toward the ex-spouse or third party have no impact *on them* at all. Typically, exes don't know or care what you think. If they feel guilty for their actions, it is because of what they did, not because of you. Your lack of forgiveness eats *you* up—and only you. It steals *your* joy and keeps *you* tied to the one you can't stand—and to the past.

In the stories, you saw shame, blame, guilt, and a sense of failure, all of which prevented these people from gaining closure. When a spouse dies, there is closure because the person is gone, but in divorce your ex is still around to haunt you mentally or even physically. If you feel encroached on by your ex, it's only because you're letting him or her have this power over you. It's far better to decide to forgive your ex, forgive any third-party "other woman/man," and forgive yourself.

Why Is Forgiveness So Tough?

Forgiveness is a decision, and it's rarely an easy one. Some of us find it hard to forgive an ex. But if you understand some of the reasons why you won't forgive, you may be able to break the stranglehold that unforgiveness has on you.

Pride. One cause of being unable to forgive is pride. You know you were right and your ex was wrong. And this may be very true. But both of you played a role in whatever happened that divided you. Although it's hard to drop the prideful stance, remember that when you are self-righteous and proud, you are stubborn. Stubbornness never serves you well. The upshot of it is that you become unwilling to even consider what is in your own best interest, and that's just foolish. Remember, *you* benefit from your forgiveness.

Revenge. If you want to get even and hurt the one who hurt you, this attitude will keep your heart in a hateful place. And revenge can lead you to do things that are self-destructive. When revenge is the motive, you never help yourself.

Bitterness. Anger, resentment, and bitterness go together. Don't let a root of bitterness develop in your heart because it will destroy you. The only person injured when you are bitter is you. The person you're mad at doesn't know or care you're fuming inside. Nor does he or she know about your rage or feel your resentment. And telling your ex-spouse accomplishes nothing. The only cure? Pull out the root of bitterness and get on with feeling better.

It has been said that life is 10 percent what happens to me and 90 percent how I react to it. Bad things do happen to good people, but they only cripple us if we let them.

Unforgiveness Is Bondage

Someone who is in bondage is a slave, a person in subjugation to an outside force. That sums up the essence of unforgiveness. You grant your ex-spouse the ability to keep you tied up in knots. You give him or her the power to control your emotions. You allow him or her to dominate your thinking and actions. Resentment keeps you under the control of the person you resent. By holding on to pain and hate, you're holding on to the person who hurt you, and that's just not smart. You cannot put that ex behind you, get free of him or her, or get closure until you forgive. Once you do, then you are free.

Forgiveness Doesn't Mean Condoning

Remember, you're definitely not trying to pretend that what your ex did to you was okay. Forgiving someone does not require you to condone disrespect or cruel actions or tolerate them. If what your ex did was immoral, it still is. If what she did was mean-spirited, forgiving her doesn't change that. You don't have to forget, and you don't have to believe it was anything other than what it was. What you have to do is decide to give up the anger and vindication. Get to a place where the pain is gone and you're free from the bondage of bitterness.

Unforgiveness Wastes Your Time

Make a list of what you accomplish by anger, hate, resentment, and time spent thinking and talking about your ex. Believe us, you'll come up with only one word—nothing. Unforgiveness wastes your time, gets you nowhere, and produces nothing but frustration.

When you need a moment of comfort, take a look at a shortened version of the Serenity Prayer that is a staple of those who are in Alcoholics Anonymous:

> God grant me the serenity
> to accept the things I cannot change;
> the courage to change the things I can;
> and the wisdom to know the difference.

The past is passed, and we cannot change it. You can, however, identify the things you can change—yourself and your relationships with others—and have the courage to change those. If you can, you'll achieve greater serenity in life.

Forgiveness Allows You to Trust and Love

When you are tormented by what someone has done to you, it is impossible for you to trust and be open with others. You have to get past the hurts to see that not everyone is like the one who injured you. Risks are unavoidable because love requires some vulnerability. But you can't truly be vulnerable and open when you're still smarting from a wound to the heart. We are supposed to love others in the same way we love ourselves (Matthew 22:39). And you know you can't do that and be bitter toward someone at the same time. Nor can you start a new relationship and keep your bitterness from spilling out.

Unforgiveness Is Baggage

Divorced people have a lot of baggage that gets in the way of making a remarriage work. Especially harmful is unforgiveness. Have you ever been around a person who talks about nothing but the wrongs someone did to him or her? Do you know someone who was wounded in a relationship and has buried the pain inside? Would you want to marry someone who was spending time and energy stewing about his or her ex-spouse? Before you can move into the next marriage, you have to let go of the last one.

Unforgiveness Invites Temptation

Being in a state of anger, resentment, and bitterness is a prescription for opening the door to trouble. When are you most vulnerable to doing something wrong or stupid? It's *not* when you are happy and peaceful. Here are some times when you get into trouble:

- When something stirs you up.
- When the status quo isn't good enough.
- When you want to act out against someone.
- When you're determined to show your ex.
- When you want revenge and want to hurt your ex for what he or she did.

None of these things produces feelings of tranquility. None gets you closure.

Forgiveness Heals

Scientific studies show conclusively that forgiveness improves your emotional and physical state of health. Immune system malfunctioning, high blood pressure, and other measurable health factors are affected by the trifecta of unforgiveness: hostility, anger, and stress.

Ways to Forgive

If you decide today that you want to forgive your ex, use the following tips to help you achieve that goal. It won't happen instantly. You can't just will it, and just saying it doesn't make it so. But deciding you will accomplish the task is a great start. Walk through these important steps.

Remember the good as well as the bad. At some time during your marriage, some wonderful things probably happened. Just because the marriage eventually went sour doesn't mean it was a mistake. A woman in our divorce recovery program had been married 45 years and had six grown children and nine grandchildren. She told how her marriage had been wonderful until her husband went off the deep end and decided to have a mistress. At first, during this woman's angry period, she called the marriage "a big mistake." She wondered how she could have been taken in by him. But later, upon reflection, she said she would never trade those years and the wonderful parts of it, especially her children and grandchildren. This process helped ease her hatred of her wayward husband.

Admit your role. Figure out what you did to contribute to the outcome, even if it was just ignoring obvious warning signs that something bad could happen. When you decide to take a more objective look at your marriage, you're less likely to have such hostile feelings. Most divorced people do reach a point a number of years after the divorce when they no longer feel pain, and they see more clearly what each person did in the marriage.

Empathize with your ex. Imagine that you're your ex-spouse. Role-play that you're now in his or her position. What is he going through? What problems does he now face? What does his future look like? Go over all of these issues, and you may decide you're happy that you're not in his shoes. Your ex has a great deal of turmoil going on that caused him to behave the way he did. He may even have serious problems. Recognize that he has lost something, too—you as a friend, at the very least. When someone tells us that he was on the losing end of the divorce deal and that the ex has it made, we know better. No one comes out a winner in a divorce. And you never know what problems your ex is facing. Typically, when you see an ex, that person tries to put on a good face, but don't believe it. Divorce hurt your ex, too.

Let go of anger and retribution. Don't dwell on either. A simple way is to change the channel. Select a substitute subject or thought. When negative thoughts about your ex creep into your mind, consciously shift your thinking to this new subject. Think instead about a trip you're planning, or your child's poem she wrote you, or your thankfulness for all the positive people in your life. Each time you start thinking, "That nasty ex of mine cheated on me, and now he's out having fun with his new girlfriend," immediately shift your mind to the vacation, poem, or the positive people. Don't let the bad thoughts invade your life and upset you. With this method, you'll notice that the bad thoughts will occur less and less frequently.

Ask God to help you with your decision to forgive. Pray for God's help in forgiving. Jesus said, "If you forgive those who sin against you, your heavenly Father will forgive you. But if you refuse to forgive others, your Father will not forgive your sins" (Matthew 6:14-15 NLT).

Forgiveness is a process that takes time to accomplish fully. Don't be upset if you backslide into old feelings now and then. At first, you may be just going through the motions of saying you forgive. But if you allow yourself the time and want to succeed, you will.

Ask your ex for forgiveness or apologize. We know this is tough, but it's one of the best ways to get closure. If you cannot bring yourself to confront your ex head-on, write a letter. Keep in mind that you are doing this for *you*. End the discussion with the words you intend to say: "I am sorry for my role in our divorce. Will you please forgive me?" It doesn't matter how or even if your ex responds. She may be humble and ask you for forgiveness as well. He may say he accepts your forgiveness. She may be mute. Or your ex may get mad and try to pull you into a fight. Don't get drawn in. Remain calm and don't comment on how your ex responds. You've accomplished your job when you ask for forgiveness. It's over.

In one of Ed's marriages, his ex-wife gave him a tape in which she apologized and detailed her role in the breakup. "She told me she did this because she knew she might later say something contrary when she was feeling a twinge of pain. But this way I would always have her apology, and she couldn't take it back. I can't tell you how much I appreciated the gesture. It was not what she said on the tape that mattered. It was the fact that she said it. That is what will matter to you, too. You will have a sense of relief and release when you forgive."

Forgiving Yourself

Beyond forgiving others is the critical task of forgiving yourself. In spite of what we tell others, we all feel somewhat guilty for the failure of a marriage. Maybe you did something you're not proud of. You mentally abused your spouse. You were unfaithful. You developed an addiction. Whatever it was, sometimes it is hard to forgive yourself. Ed says, "Even after my ex forgave me, I couldn't seem to forgive myself. But I do have a little advice here. I asked God to forgive me, and that's the only way I know that works."

Get a Future

Now that you have achieved closure in your divorce, begin living in the present and planning your future. This requires setting some goals; otherwise you're aimless. Any positive direction will do.

In Jim's book *Growing Through Divorce*, he recommends setting goals in ten areas:

- *Relational goals:* What do you want to do about friends and family?

- *Personal goals:* What do you want to accomplish now as a single person?

- *Vocational goals:* What will you do with yourself in work, volunteering, etc.?

- *Spiritual goals:* Knowing divorce can strengthen or weaken you spiritually, what will you do now?

- *Financial goals:* What do you need to do to feel more comfortable about money?

- *Educational goals:* No matter what age you are, you may want to get more education.

- *Family goals:* What goals do you want to set for your children or what do you want to do with them?

- *Health goals:* What will you do to enhance your physical health?

- *Sexual goals:* You're divorced, but still kicking. What choices are right for you?

- *Emotional goals:* Where are you emotionally? Where do you want to be?[1]

Your plans should be independent of remarriage. Who knows the future? Devise a life plan that depends only on you. If things change, you can adjust your plans.

How will you know when you're "whole"? You have closure with the past. You are functioning in the present in all respects. You have plans. No longer are you vulnerable to marrying the wrong person for the wrong reasons.

20
The Ready2Remarry Test

❧ ❧ ❧

It is not a lack of love, but a lack of friendship that makes unhappy marriages.

FRIEDRICH NIETZSCHE

Two things that go hand in hand are recovering from divorce and lowering your vulnerability to remarrying the wrong person for the wrong reasons. Both take time. Since this is a process with two steps forward and one step back, you need to monitor your progress routinely. One way you can do that is by "taking your temperature" using the Ready2Remarry Test. This simple checklist deals with issues regarding recovery and your proclivity to being vulnerable. Gauging where you are will help you see your progress over time and clarify areas in which you still need work. If you find yourself stuck in certain respects, seek help from others who have been through divorce or from a family counselor.

Since your goal is to become a healthy, functioning, whole person, you must be willing to work at it and check your progress.

And don't jump to the conclusion that if you score well that means you should run out and get married. But also don't seriously consider remarriage until you find that you're doing well on all of these factors. When you can truly say to yourself that you're happy in your present circumstances and you're not looking for another person to make you complete or solve your problems, you are indeed in the best possible position. If you meet someone you want to marry, that's great. But if you don't, the lack of a partner will be no problem for you because you're fine as you are.

The most critical issues in the test arise from things we have already emphasized:

- Have you allowed enough time to heal by going through all the emotional stages following divorce?
- Have you become independent in your financial situation and parenting life?
- Have you developed a satisfying social life of friends and activities?
- Have your children had time to heal and adjust?
- Are you strong enough to take care of someone else rather than just expecting someone to save you?
- Are you marrying out of desire rather than need or desperation?

How to Take the Ready2Remarry (R2R) Test

Make a number of copies of the pages of the R2R Test. Use one and set aside the others for later.

Take the test. Answer honestly. See how you did. Work on areas where you scored less than a five on each question.

Wait a few months and take it again. Don't look back at your previous answers until you have answered the questions the second time. Then compare answers to see where you are making progress and where you are stuck. Devote extra time to problem issues by asking yourself why you're not progressing and what's impeding your progress. Do you need to change your attitude? Do you need to change your behavior? Do you need to take steps to prevent your ex from having a negative impact on you? Are other people getting in the way of your recovery? Analyze what's wrong and devise a plan to make changes so you will improve. This is growing by learning.

Testing the Other Person

When you become involved with someone you're interested in marrying, have him or her take the test…or take it for him or her. If your fiancé is not ready and wants to marry you for the wrong reasons, the marriage may fail even though you're in a good place. Why be a victim because of someone else's problems?

Ready2Remarry Test

	Describes me Very well—Not at all				
	5	4	3	2	1
Emotional					
No longer in denial about my divorce	❑	❑	❑	❑	❑
Have mourned the loss of my marriage	❑	❑	❑	❑	❑
Allowed enough time to grieve/recover (two years or more)	❑	❑	❑	❑	❑
Don't feel overwhelmed by responsibilities	❑	❑	❑	❑	❑
Free of excessive fears and anxiety	❑	❑	❑	❑	❑
No addictions to alcohol, drugs, or prescription medicines	❑	❑	❑	❑	❑
Balanced spiritually, psychologically, and mentally	❑	❑	❑	❑	❑
Have let go of anger, resentments, hostilities, and mistrust	❑	❑	❑	❑	❑
Have no desire to prove something or get revenge against ex	❑	❑	❑	❑	❑

	Describes me Very well—Not at all				
	5	4	3	2	1
Have stopped talking all the time about my divorce	☐	☐	☐	☐	☐
Am no longer feeling like a victim	☐	☐	☐	☐	☐
Have mentally and physically let go of ex	☐	☐	☐	☐	☐
Have no feelings of desperation	☐	☐	☐	☐	☐
Have made progress toward forgiving ex	☐	☐	☐	☐	☐
Feel a sense of peace and stability in my life	☐	☐	☐	☐	☐

Financial

	5	4	3	2	1
Have established own accounts, credit, etc.	☐	☐	☐	☐	☐
Am out of debt or have a functioning plan to accomplish it	☐	☐	☐	☐	☐
Am financially stable (for at least 18 months)	☐	☐	☐	☐	☐
Not in search of a financial savior	☐	☐	☐	☐	☐
Have resolved all major legal issues in my divorce	☐	☐	☐	☐	☐
Have my career on track or am progressing toward it	☐	☐	☐	☐	☐

Social

	5	4	3	2	1
Have lived without live-in lovers or parents (two years or more)	☐	☐	☐	☐	☐
Have a stable set of true friends, acquaintances, and supporters— single and married	☐	☐	☐	☐	☐

	Describes me Very well—Not at all				
	5	4	3	2	1
Have dropped all negative people	☐	☐	☐	☐	☐
Am not feeling lonely all the time	☐	☐	☐	☐	☐
Have an active social life	☐	☐	☐	☐	☐
Have hobbies and interests that are fulfilling	☐	☐	☐	☐	☐

Parental

Have worked out arrangements about children with ex	☐	☐	☐	☐	☐
Am taking care of children without need for a spouse	☐	☐	☐	☐	☐
Am not in search of a coparenting savior	☐	☐	☐	☐	☐

Learning

Have learned what my role was in marriage breakup	☐	☐	☐	☐	☐
Have assumed responsibility for what I did that led to the divorce	☐	☐	☐	☐	☐

Future

Have a life plan involving relational, personal, vocational, spiritual, financial, educational, family, health, sexual, and emotional goals	☐	☐	☐	☐	☐
Have evolved a clear idea of my life purpose and am pursuing it	☐	☐	☐	☐	☐

Living Situation

Am not living "in sin" so that guilt becomes a factor in marital decision	☐	☐	☐	☐	☐

	Describes me Very well — Not at all				
	5	4	3	2	1
Do not have my ex as part of my day-to-day life	☐	☐	☐	☐	☐
Am living in the present now, not in the past	☐	☐	☐	☐	☐

Attitude Toward Remarriage

	5	4	3	2	1
Believe single life can be as happy as married life	☐	☐	☐	☐	☐
Have achieved enough self-confidence to avoid the need to rescue or be rescued	☐	☐	☐	☐	☐
Want to have a marriage partner, but don't need to have one	☐	☐	☐	☐	☐
Have no timetable for remarrying	☐	☐	☐	☐	☐
Am not overly craving romance	☐	☐	☐	☐	☐
Have identified the healthy, personal needs a committed relationship would fill	☐	☐	☐	☐	☐
Am ready to take care of someone else (not just be taken care of)	☐	☐	☐	☐	☐
Am not expecting someone to make my life exciting	☐	☐	☐	☐	☐
I feel like I can trust my judgment	☐	☐	☐	☐	☐

Dating

	5	4	3	2	1
Have dated enough potential partners to determine what I want and don't want	☐	☐	☐	☐	☐
Have a clear profile of what a new spouse should be like	☐	☐	☐	☐	☐

	Describes me Very well—Not at all				
	5	4	3	2	1
Am not focused on only one or a few traits that are opposite from ex	☐	☐	☐	☐	☐
Have rejected "soul mate mentality" that can cause lack of objectivity in evaluating prospects	☐	☐	☐	☐	☐
Am not subject to or have learned to resist marriage pressures from friends, family, or dating partner	☐	☐	☐	☐	☐
Am not desperately wishing dating life would end	☐	☐	☐	☐	☐

Prospective Remarriage Partner

	5	4	3	2	1
Have a prospective partner I've dated in a committed relationship for at least two years	☐	☐	☐	☐	☐
Have a strong friendship with prospective partner	☐	☐	☐	☐	☐
Am in love with him/her	☐	☐	☐	☐	☐
Don't expect to change him/her in order to be happy	☐	☐	☐	☐	☐
Have tested potential partner to see how he or she would perform in a parental role	☐	☐	☐	☐	☐
Feel no obligation to marry this person	☐	☐	☐	☐	☐
Have become familiar with his/her family and friends	☐	☐	☐	☐	☐
Have made a list of this person's negatives and not overlooked problems	☐	☐	☐	☐	☐

21
What's Stopping You?

❧ ❧ ❧

There's only one way to have
a happy marriage and as soon as I learn
what it is, I'll get married again.

CLINT EASTWOOD

Okay, you passed the Ready2Remarry Test. You're really in a good place to consider remarrying. You have a full life and feel no pressure to remarry, but you're fretting about it. With all you've been through with your divorce, it's normal for you be a little fearful about taking a chance and loving again.

And we're sure we haven't made it any easier with all our emphasis on remarrying for the wrong reasons. But take heart! We believe in marriage! We recognize that there are factors that might make you afraid to remarry when you are healed from your divorce and should be ready to consider another march down the aisle. Getting remarried requires vulnerability and taking a risk. We believe love is worth it. Maybe we can lessen your hesitancy if we take a look at some wrong reasons for not remarrying.

You may have decided, legitimately, that you would be happier staying single. This is a wise decision if you truly know that marriage is just not for you. You could decide that remarriage would make your life too complicated. Maybe you realize that you prefer the single life. Your family may be so important to you that you know you don't have the time or energy to put into another marriage. You may sense that you have a selfish streak and that you are unwilling to share and give enough to make a marriage work. Maybe you've been divorced multiple times and now believe you are not cut out for marital relationships.

You're not alone if you choose not to remarry. Ten percent of adults never marry. Of those who marry and divorce, 20 percent never remarry. For some, marriage is not right or the timing is not right.

On the other hand, there are some not-so-good reasons that may cause you to hold back even when you are ready to remarry. These reasons could be barriers to your having a happier life. Because of that, we'll touch on a few of them so you can reflect on whether you are using any of these as excuses for not opening yourself up to the possibility of remarrying.

Remarriage Stoppers

Fear of Repeat Failure

There is one thing worse than getting a divorce: Getting two divorces. Divorce may leave you in the situation where you feel like a personal failure. You blame yourself, no matter who left. It's scary to think, "I could remarry and get divorced again." This fear of failing may prevent you from even getting out and dating. Remember the movie about the runaway bride? She got so close to the altar but panicked at the last minute. But with your new knowledge from this book, the odds are in your favor. Take a chance.

Not Marriage Material

It's easy to believe after getting a divorce, "I am just not marriage material." We hear this all the time from people who conclude that their unhappy marriage was due to their own natures. It's a very common feeling. You will begin to have some perspective on your failed marriage after a period of time and realize that "not being marriage material" wasn't the reason the marriage failed. And, remember, you are unlikely to have the same interactions with the next person you marry. The problems in your previous marriage may not happen in the next one, especially if you have learned from the role you played by growing through your divorce. The reality is that when you do not have a marriage prospect, marriage seems unlikely. However, when you meet a special person, everything can change and you suddenly feel like marriage material again!

Fear of Dating

Just as the fear of dating can drive some people to remarry in order to avoid having to date, others never get that far. They never get started. They think of dating as something for 17 year olds, and they want no part of it. If this describes you, realize that dating is nothing more than letting yourself be exposed to various people who could become good friends. In some cases, maybe more. If you are ready to remarry, don't let the fear of dating bar you from expanding your social life and possibly meeting someone you might consider as your next spouse.

Can't Find Mr./Ms. Perfect

Another remarriage stopper is the search for Mr. or Ms. Perfect. Since the first marriage didn't work out and the ex had lots of flaws, you think the solution is to find someone who has none. Good luck. Everybody has baggage and flaws. Not settling for just anyone is good advice. Setting your standards so high that no one can match up is unwise. Take a look at yourself and ask what your "disadvantages" are that a prospective mate might see. Now, give some slack to other people, recognizing that you could be happy with someone who is not perfect.

I'm Flawed

This is the opposite of refusing to consider remarrying unless someone is perfect. In this case, you decide you are damaged goods. The divorce branded you. Who would want you? Why even try to find another mate? If you feel like you're just not good enough or that you are a loser because of your divorce, you will resist considering remarriage. Hopefully you have recovered from such thinking by now. If you haven't, give yourself a break and recognize there is someone for almost everyone. The proof is that 90 percent marry, and 80 percent of divorced people remarry.

Fear of Being Taken to the Cleaners

You got a big settlement from your divorce or your ex-spouse took you to the cleaners and finally you have recovered financially. You don't want to lose what you've got now in another divorce. That's a common concern for people who have money or who lost it in a divorce. You can love money, but it can't love you back. Don't let fear of losing money stop you from remarrying. There are plenty of ways to legally protect yourself in the next marriage. Consult an attorney if you are worried about it.

Had the Love of My Life

Some people believe their first husband/wife was their one chance for love. It's over now. That's it. No more chances! This is nonsense. Ask the many people who are remarried, and most will tell you they are as much in love (or more so) than they were the first time. There is more than one person in the world to whom you could be happily married.

No One Can Match Up to My Ex

My ex was perfect. He left me and nobody else will ever be like him. That's true. No one else will be like your ex. But you got a divorce, and there must have been a reason. He couldn't have been that great. Don't put on rose-colored glasses about the past. It's history. Even if the next person doesn't match up exactly, if you give someone else a chance, you may be pleasantly surprised.

My Children Hate Whomever I Date

I can't remarry. My kids won't let me. Yes, sometimes children do control adults—if we let them. You need to help your children understand and adjust to new people in your life. Don't allow their fears and feelings to stop you from having the future you want.

Remarrying for the wrong reasons increases your risk of another divorce. Not remarrying for the reasons just mentioned may limit your chance for happiness as a married person again. Choose wisely.

Partner Pickers

If you're serious about finding a marriage partner, you may have used or considered using one of the Internet matchmaking services. One of the most popular Internet matchmaking websites is eHarmony. com. The founder, Dr. Neil Clark Warren, has the same objective that we do—lowering the divorce rate in America. His notion is that people make bad choices in mate selection because they use the wrong criteria. "People tend to fall in love for all the wrong reasons. Physical appearance, power, prestige, social status, wealth and sexual chemistry are a few of the more transient, fickle qualities on which men and women sometimes base their relationships."

Here is how his belief and ours are the same: Divorces occur because people remarry the wrong person. We believe this occurs when you are not healed from your divorce and are not ready to remarry. As a result, you marry for the wrong reasons. Dr. Warren concurs, but thinks the problem is that people don't know how to choose a mate using the qualities that are important.

Dr. Warren believes that if you match up on 29 dimensions of "compatibility" with another person, you have a chance of finding your soul mate. These 29 dimensions were extracted from surveys of married couples. When couples matched up on these 29, they tended to be very happily married. When they didn't match well, they tended to be unhappy in their marriages. Thus, he assumes that if you can find a mate who matches you in these areas, you have a much greater chance of being happily married, too. For Dr. Warren, his use of the term "soul mate" means a person you are extremely compatible with on all 29 dimensions. This is not the way the general public or we use the term.

The underlying philosophy of Internet matchmaking is that the companies have a huge pool of potential prospects to introduce to you. In contrast, your own circle of friends is likely too small to include someone who is your perfect match.

Should you use Internet services? We know people who have had success and some who have not. Here are the pros and cons.

Benefits

- Widens your options of people to consider.

- Introduces you to people who are largely serious about marriage (otherwise they wouldn't fill out that lengthy questionnaire). Some Internet sites are just meat markets, however.

- Can screen people who do match you on a number of important criteria.

- Offers you many people to consider. They don't assume that anyone who matches you will automatically be someone you would choose.

Cautions

- Is not a proven system yet. While the 29 dimensions that eHarmony.com identified did discriminate between happily and unhappily married couples, this correlation doesn't prove that it will work in reducing the rate of divorce. It will take 10 to 15 years to see if those people who met using this system have a lower divorce rate than people of the same age who met in more traditional ways.

- Is based on surveys. As a survey expert for 35 years, Ed can say without hesitation that on sensitive or loaded subject areas, many people lie. These matchmaking services rely on people answering the questionnaire truthfully. Many will not.

Bottom line? No matchmaking service can offer you a happy marriage if you or your "intended" is marrying for the wrong reasons. If you have not taken the time and effort to heal from your divorce and develop a full life without marriage, you risk making a remarriage mistake. If you are marriage-ready, matchmaking services can expand your options and help you better understand who you are and the type of person you should be seeking. Still, just because someone matches you on various dimensions doesn't mean this is the right individual for you. And since people may lie when they respond to the matchmaking questionnaire, you have to have a "buyer beware" attitude. Don't jump into any marriage. Watch for red flags. Bail if he or she is the wrong person. Take your time. Don't give up.

22
You Are Not Alone!

❧ ❧ ❧

Love may be blind,
but marriage is a real eye-opener!

One thing we've learned from talking to a lot of divorced people—
they are very confused about the facts about divorce and remarriage.
They feel they are all alone in getting a divorce, and no one else
has a situation like theirs. They hear all sorts of horror stories and
supposed facts that discourage them. Over time we have cataloged
some of the myths.

These myths can do real damage. If, for example, you believe
you have little chance of finding someone to date or remarry, you
may not even try. Other myths can lead you to overlook useful facts
that would have altered your behavior if you had just known about
them. Knowledge is power, so don't get thrown off by tales you hear
circulating from uninformed people.

We would like to clear up some of these untruths for you. Using
recent data from the Census Bureau and the National Center for

Health Statistics, we will debunk the junk. While you may think statistics are dry stuff, you will find these facts encouraging.

Myth 1: The vast majority of adults in America are married.

False. Half of the population is currently married and living with their spouses. Yes, you read correctly; half of all adults in America are single, divorced, or widowed. There is a small percentage who are separated or not living with their spouses. You are not alone. There are millions of people just like you who are potential single friends and remarriage candidates.

Myth 2: Most available single (never married) people are very young.

This used to be true, but not anymore. There are a lot of single marriage prospects even in the 35-and-over age group. First time marriage in America is changing dramatically. It was common as late as the 1970s that people got married right out of high school. The median age at which women got married in 1970 was 20.8 years. In 2003, it was 25.3 years. During that same time period, the median age of first marriage for men rose from 23.2 to 27.1. Today's younger adults are waiting longer to marry to get an education and establish a career. Also, changing attitudes about cohabitation, the reality of children born out of wedlock, and the widespread availability of birth control have been factors in removing the earlier motivation to marry while very young. Another factor may be the realization by some that their parents' early marriages often led to divorce. Whether by fear or wisdom, today's younger generations are avoiding what they may view as their parents' mistakes. Fully a third of men and almost a quarter of women ages 30 to 34 have yet to get married. Even a sizable number of people in the 35 to 44 age group are still unmarried—20 percent of men and 13 percent of women.

Myth 3: There are not many divorced and widowed people to date in my age group.

Well, there are 21 million divorced and 14 million widowed people in the country, so if you aren't finding anyone to date, you aren't looking very hard. True, some have no interest in dating or mating. Still, there are a lot of people like you in every age group.

Note in the following table that there are 8.9 million men and 12.7 million women who are currently divorced. There are 2.7 million men and 11.3 million women who are widowed. The majority of divorced people are in the age ranges of 35 to 54. The vast majority of widowed are age 65 and over. Still there are substantial numbers in *every* age category, although the ratio of men to women gets thin for older folks.

Percentage divorced and widowed by age			
Men divorced	Men widowed	Women divorced	Women widowed
8.9 million	2.7 million	12.7 million	11.3 million
%	%	%	%
15-19			
0	0	0	0
20-24			
1	0	1	0
25-29			
4	0	4	0
30-34			
8	1	7	0
35-44			
26	3	26	3
45-54			
31	7	29	6
55-64			
19	11	20	13
65 & over			
11	77	13	77

Myth 4: Divorce rates are increasing.

During the past 30 years divorce rates have increased. Census studies reveal that almost 50 percent of first marriages eventually end in divorce. In fact, divorce has become so common that for every two people getting married, there is one person getting a divorce (7.4 marriages and 3.8 divorces for every 1000 people each year). However, the divorce rate has stabilized in recent years and may actually be declining.

There are some characteristics that have been determined to be related to higher odds of getting a divorce:

- Those who get married at a younger age.
- Those who have a lower education.
- Those who have a premarital birth.
- Those who have premarital sexual activity.

These factors that are correlated with higher divorce rates do not prove that these are causes of divorce. In fact, they may be related to a causal issue such as immaturity or a lack of responsibility. Nevertheless, when people marry at a young age (under 25), the odds of marital dissolution are higher. The delay of first marriage by today's younger generations bodes well for the likelihood that these groups will face a lower rate of divorce.

Myth 5: Most divorces occur after many years of marriage.

Even though there have been press articles that grandpa and grandma are now divorcing after 35 years, more than half of all first marriages that end in divorce take place within the first 8 years. The median duration of first marriages that end in divorce is 7.8 years for men and 7.9 years for women.

The median duration of second marriages that end in divorce is even shorter: 7.3 years for men and 6.8 years for women. These short-lived marriages reflect the realities discussed in this book. When you marry or remarry for the wrong reasons, the problems surface early and maintaining the marriage becomes difficult. As a result, these DOA marriages end relatively quickly.

Myth 6: Living with someone prior to marriage reduces the odds of getting another divorce.

Sounds reasonable. Most believe it. But it is bunk. If you are thinking about living with someone before marrying to lower your chance of another divorce, forget it.

Living together (unmarried cohabitation) has grown considerably in recent years. In 1996, the percentage of households that classified themselves as unmarried partners (living with someone of the opposite sex identified as an unmarried partner) was about 3 percent. By 2003,

4 percent, or 4.6 million households, were classified as unmarried partners. This may be understated since some people may not want to admit it to the census takers. In these unmarried partner households, 41 percent had children under 18 living with them.

Living together arrangements overall are less stable than marriages. The probability of a first marriage ending in a breakup (separation or divorce) within 5 years is 20 percent, within 10 years, 31 percent. For unmarried partners living together, the odds of breaking up within 5 years are 49 percent, within 10 years 62 percent. Part of the rationale people give for living together prior to marriage is so they can "test" the relationship, and if it doesn't work out, it is easier to break up from a live-in situation than from a legal marriage. This isn't true from an emotional point of view.

Also, many studies have shown that couples who lived together prior to marriage have a higher rate of divorce once married than those who did not live together. Does living together increase the likelihood of divorce? The argument that "playing house" offers a chance to improve mate selection and provide premarital experience to minimize the chance of divorce turns out to be untrue. Note that we are *not* stating an ethical opinion. These are facts taken from statistical studies showing that those who live together before marriage have a much higher rate of divorce. A study conducted by Yale and Columbia universities concluded that "the dissolution rate of women who cohabit premaritally with their future spouse is, on average, nearly 80 percent higher than the rate of those who do not."

What are the explanations for this counterintuitive outcome? What one group of researchers found was that those living together before marriage had lower levels of marital interaction and higher levels of marital disagreement and marital instability. Another researcher believed that people who choose to live together are less likely to prefer relationships that are permanent and, therefore, are more likely to divorce. Our theory is that if you prefer to live with someone rather than marry him or her in order to "test out" the relationship, you are already skeptical that this is the right person for you and that it will work. Your initial instincts were probably correct, so that when you did marry, it proved what you expected and didn't work. The Bible has taught for thousands of years that marriage is the best way. Not surprisingly, history has confirmed this wisdom to be true.

Myth 7: The odds of your remarrying are slim.

The vast majority of divorced people remarry. In one study of women who were divorced, 54 percent remarried within 5 years and 75 percent remarried within 10 years. If a women was younger (under the age of 25) when she was divorced, her odds of remarrying were even higher—81 percent in 10 years. Women over age 25 when divorced had a 68 percent likelihood of remarriage in 10 years. If you choose to remarry, the odds are even better than these statistics because some divorced men and women decide after trying marriage that they want no part of it. Marriage is not for them, so they never remarry by choice.

However, as many of the survey stories in this book revealed, people often choose to remarry too quickly and live to regret it. The study of divorced women referenced showed that 15 percent remarried in 1 year and 39 percent within 3 years. Some anecdotal evidence about men suggests they remarry even more hastily.

Myth 8: Few people get divorced more than once.

Not true. That's the reason we wrote this book. Far too many people get divorced multiple times. We know that the divorce rate for second marriages is 40 percent within 10 years. Some evidence suggests it eventually goes as high as 60 percent. As we saw earlier, second marriages end in divorce even more quickly than failed first marriages. Clearly, many have not learned how to avoid a repeat performance.

A recent study of divorced women who remarried within 5 years found 23 percent ended in separation or divorce within 5 years after that remarriage and 39 percent within 10 years. Interestingly, there were certain conditions that increased the chance that a remarriage would end. The researchers concluded that 32 percent of these second marriages broke up within 10 years if neither one of the couple had children at the time of remarriage. In contrast, if either or both of the couple had children where none were unwanted, the odds of breakup were 40 percent. In remarriages where an unwanted child belonged to either party at the time of remarriage, the second marriage broke up 44 percent of the time.

Another factor that led to differences in the likelihood of redivorce was age at time of remarriage. For those women who remarried when they were under age 25, the odds of another breakup within 10 years was 47 percent. For women who remarried when they were 25 or older, 34 percent broke up within 10 years. Remarrying younger increases the chance of getting another divorce.

Why Remarry?

Why are people motivated to continue marrying? Is it the triumph of hope over experience? Statistical data clearly demonstrate that those who are married have some significant advantages over those who are unmarried.

Compared with unmarried men and women, married people tend to have higher-age mortality, have less risky behavior patterns, higher sexual frequency, more satisfaction with their sexual lives, more savings, and higher wages. In contrast, divorced persons have lower levels of psychological well being, have a greater risk of early mortality, have more social isolation, less satisfying sexual lives, more negative life events, greater levels of depression and alcohol use, and higher levels of unhappiness and self-acceptance. These are statistical tendencies, and do not describe all people. Many married people are miserable and many divorced are delirious. If you have been married and divorced, you understand this. But these statistical findings support what many people believe: You would be better off and happier long-term if you were married—*when* you are ready and to the *right* person in the *right* circumstances.

Some Key Points to Remember

- The seeds of divorce are often found in the reasons people marry and remarry.
- When people make bad choices, they can expect bad outcomes.
- Remarry for the wrong reasons, and the marriage is likely to be DOA.
- Be certain your "intended spouse" is not getting married for the wrong reasons. It takes two healthy people to have a healthy marriage. If you choose to marry a person who is still in turmoil, you will get turmoil.
- Biology tends to trump logic. Once you're deeply and emotionally involved, it's extremely difficult to think clearly.
- If you feel like you *need* to remarry, don't.
- Beware of a savior looking to pull you out of your despair and hardships.
- Can two people in crisis solve their problems by joining together? In marriage, two halves don't make a whole. Two incomplete people coming together don't make them complete.
- Marry from strength rather than weakness.
- Don't remarry to make a point or prove something.
- Don't remarry to solve the problem of the "missing parent," "the depleted bank account," or the "fear of being single and dating."
- If a bell goes off telling you "it's time" to marry, ignore it.
- Don't confuse similar backgrounds, conditions, and problems with shared interests, dreams, and goals.
- When you feel like anybody will do, don't do anything with anybody.

- If you feel "less than," you will be willing to settle for someone "less than."
- Marathon dating or dating with a mission signals an unhealed divorce.
- *You* have the responsibility to make yourself happy.
- When you are blinded by love, you are blind.
- Choose your next spouse. Don't just allow yourself to be chosen.
- Bad things do happen to good people, but they cripple you only if you choose to let them.
- If you stay a victim, you will never learn what truly happened in your marriage.
- You can't rush healing after open-heart surgery, and you can't rush healing from broken-heart misery.
- The victim of your hate, bitterness, resentment, and unforgiveness is you.
- If you are not ready to take care of someone else, then take care of yourself first.
- Marriages succeed when each party is ready to give more than they get.

Notes

❧ ❧ ❧

Introduction

1. Phillip C. McGraw, *Relationship Rescue* (New York: Hyperion, 2000), pp. 6-9.

2. Dr. Neil Clark Warren, *Falling in Love for All the Right Reasons* (New York: Center Street, 2005), pp. 2-3.

Chapter 19—Get Whole!

1. Jim Smoke, *Growing Through Divorce* (Eugene, OR: Harvest House Publishers, 1995), pp. 131-43.

Recommended Reading
and Statistical Sources

❧ ❧ ❧

Books

Ahrons, Constance. *The Good Divorce*. HarperCollins Perennial, 1998.

Berry, Dawn Bradley. *The Divorce Recovery Sourcebook*. Lowell House, 1998.

Burns, Bob, and Tom Whiteman. *The Fresh Start Divorce Recovery Workbook*. Thomas Nelson, 1998.

Estess, Patricia Schiff. *Money Advice for Your Successful Remarriage: Handling Delicate Financial Issues with Love and Understanding*. Betterway Books, 1996.

Kelly, Susan. *The Second Time Around: Everything You Need to Know to Make Your Remarriage Happy*. William Morrow, 2000.

Luskin, Dr. Fred. *Forgive for Good*. Harper-San Francisco, 2000.

Margulies, Sam. *Getting Divorced Without Ruining Your Life: A Reasoned Practical Guide to the Legal, Financial and Emotional Ins and Outs of Negotiating a Divorce Settlement*. Fireside, 2001.

Mercer, Diana, and Marsha Kline Pruett. *Your Divorce Advisor: A Lawyer and a Psychologist Guide You Through the Legal and Emotional Landscape of Divorce*. Fireside, 2001.

Smith, Gayle Rosenwald. *Divorce and Money: Everything You Need to Know*. Berkley, 2004.

Smoke, Jim. *Growing Through Divorce*. Harvest House Publishers, 1995.

———. *Seven Keys to a Healthy Blended Family*. Harvest House Publishers, 2004.

Warren, Dr. Neil Clark. *Falling in Love for All the Right Reasons*. Center Street, 2005.

Articles

Anderson, Nancy E. "Happily Ever After." *NorthShore* magazine, January 2003.

Marano, Hara Estroff. "Divorced? (remarriage in America)." *Psychology Today*. March 2000.

"When You Marry for a Reason Other Than Love." *Bonkers Magazine.* 1998.

Statistical Sources

"America's Families and Living Arrangements 2003." U.S. Department of Commerce, U.S. Bureau of the Census, November 2004.

"Births, Marriages, Divorces, and Deaths: Provisional Data for May 2004." National Vital Statistical Reports, U.S. Department of Health and Human Services, National Center for Health Statistics, Centers for Disease Control and Prevention, 2004.

"Children with single parents—how they fare." Census Brief, U.S. Department of Commerce, U.S. Bureau of the Census, 1997.

"Cohabitation, Marriage, Divorce, and Remarriage in the United States." Series 23, Number 22, National Survey of Family Growth, U.S. Department of Health and Human Services, National Center for Health Statistics, Centers for Disease Control and Prevention, July 2002.

"Marital Status: 2000." U.S. Department of Commerce, U.S. Bureau of the Census, October 2003.

"Marriage, Divorce, and Remarriage in the 1990's." U.S. Department of Commerce, U.S. Bureau of the Census, 1995.

"Remarriage and Subsequent Divorces—United States." Series 21, Number 45, U.S. Department of Health and Human Services, National Center for Health Statistics, Centers for Disease Control and Prevention, 2003.

Stanton, Glenn T. "Does Cohabitation Protect Against Divorce?" *Focus on the Family,* January 2004.

Sweeney, Megan M. "Remarriage of Men and Women: The Role of Socioeconomic Prospects." Center for Demography and Ecology, University of Wisconsin–Madison, November 1995.

To contact Edward M. Tauber or Jim Smoke,
go to their website:

www.findingtheright1.com

More than 600,000 people
have been helped by Jim Smoke's

Growing Through Divorce

**You can go through divorce or
grow through divorce!**

Shock, adjustment, mourning, and rebuilding.
Every person involved in a divorce goes through
these stages. Drawing on years of counseling
experience, Jim offers compassion, hope, and
practical steps to guide you in your divorce
recovery. You'll also discover pitfalls to avoid and
how to set attainable growth goals, including:

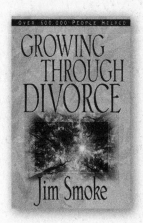

- Looking at the divorce-recovery
  process as a healing experience
- Developing a new support system
- Giving yourself the time and permission to experience
  your emotions
- Using your experience to care for, share with, and
  support others.

Joy and love can be yours again. *Growing Through Divorce* shows you how
to transform a difficult ending into a fresh beginning.

"The book that helped me most cope with the reality of divorce was
Growing Through Divorce. *This is a powerful must-read!"*

STEPHEN ARTERBURN

*"Anyone going through the divorce process will
benefit immensely from reading this resource."*

H. NORMAN WRIGHT

Seven Keys to a Healthy Blended Family

The tools you need to create a stable, happy home

Bringing two families together can be daunting. But after decades of working with divorced and remarried couples, Jim Smoke offers you time-proven principles and wisdom from God's Word to help you lay a solid foundation for your new family that includes:

- equal and fair treatment of all the children
- dealing with former spouses and their families
- integrating members of extended families
- financial considerations
- scheduling problems

With insights from parents and children in blended families, *Seven Keys to a Healthy, Blended Family* gives you practical advice and encouragement for building a positive, uplifting family life.

Other Great Books from
Harvest House Publishers

What Every Parent Needs to Know About Video Games
Richard Abanes

Packed with the latest information on the pros and cons of video and computer gaming, this concise, easy-to-follow guide helps you understand a form of entertainment that's become part of the daily lives of millions of children and adults. Bestselling author Richard Abanes—an experienced video-gamer himself—offers a great, balanced discussion.

How to Talk to Your Kids About Drugs
Stephen Arterburn and Jim Burns

With straight talk about the situations kids like yours face, bestselling authors Stephen Arterburn and Jim Burns present six key factors in drug abuse and proven techniques for prevention, the signs of drug use, and information for intervention and how to deal with kids on drugs. *How to Talk to Your Kids About Drugs* provides the knowledge and tools you need to help your kids stay or become drug-free. Includes a helpful study guide for personal use and group discussion.

Knowing God 101
Bruce Bickel and Stan Jantz

This book is brimming with joy! You'll love the inspiring descriptions of God's nature, His personality, and His activities. Curious inquirers and earnest seekers will find straightforward responses to essential questions about God, including: Eternity—where did God come from? The trinity—is God three people or one? The Bible—did God really communicate His own thoughts to us?

When Pleasing Others Is Hurting You
David Hawkins

You want to do what's right—take care of your family, be a good employee, "be there" for your friends. And everyone knows they can depend on you—so they do. But are you really doing what's best for them? And what about you? Are you happy and relaxed? Are you excited about your gifts and your calling? In this engaging book, psychologist David Hawkins shows why people feel driven to always do more. He'll help you regain vital parts of your personality and rediscover the person God created you to be.

101 Questions to Ask Before You Get Engaged
H. Norman Wright

How can I be sure? Is he (or she) really right for me? Deciding to spend the rest of your life with someone is one of the biggest decisions you'll ever make. The key to a successful marriage is getting to know your partner *before* you make the plunge. Relationship expert and noted couples counselor Norm Wright will steer you through a series of soul-searching questions—even the difficult ones that need to be addressed—to help you discern if you've met "the One."

Men Under Construction
Bob Barnes

All men are under construction—your next door neighbor…your boss…your pastor…and *you!* Wise is the man who is willing to allow his builder—God—to construct him according to His specifications. Wise also is the man willing to learn from powerful mentors—men who have walked with God through many years and have important insights to share. Bob Barnes is such a man, and in this new devotional he offers good counsel and practical insights that will help you in the areas of communicating, committing to God, pursuing honesty and integrity, and making the most of what God has given you.

500 Time-Saving Hints for Every Woman
Emilie Barnes

Bestselling author Emilie Barnes has been sharing time and sanity-saving tips with women for years. Now in this easy to use resource, Emilie reveals 500 fabulous ideas to help readers declutter their lives and homes, stop piling it and start filing it, begin each day with a To Do list, clean efficiently and effectively, and tackle projects at home and elsewhere. Every homeowner, bride, mom, and working woman will find the secrets to creating a life that has less mess and more room for what really matters.